The Flowers and Gardens of Japan

Japan is often called the land of flowers. This book gives an account of those flowers that occur in the country that are most remarkable for their beauty and profusion and that are most typically Japanese. There are also pages on landscape gardening.

WISTARIA, KYOMIDZU

The Flowers and Gardens of Japan

Ella Du Cane

LONDON AND NEW YORK

First published in 2003 by
Kegan Paul International

This edition first published in 2011 by
Routledge
2 Park Square, Milton Park, Abingdon, Oxfordshire OX14 4RN

Simultaneously published in the USA and Canada
by Routledge
711 Third Avenue, New York, NY 10017

First issued in paperback 2016

Routledge is an imprint of the Taylor & Francis Group, an informa business

© Kegan Paul, 2003

All rights reserved. No part of this book may be reprinted or reproduced or
utilised in any form or by any electronic, mechanical, or other means, now
known or hereafter invented, including photocopying and recording, or in
any information storage or retrieval system, without permission in writing
from the publishers.

British Library Cataloguing in Publication Data
A catalogue record for this book is available from the British Library

ISBN 13: 978-1-138-97441-8 (pbk)
ISBN 13: 978-0-7103-0901-3 (hbk)

Publisher's Note
The publisher has gone to great lengths to ensure the quality of this reprint
but points out that some imperfections in the original copies may be
apparent. The publisher has made every effort to contact original copyright
holders and would welcome correspondence from those they have been
unable to trace.

PREFACE

AN apology is due to the reader for adding this volume to the long list of books already written on Japan; but, being a lover of flowers myself, I found there was no book giving a short account of the flora of the country which is so often called the Land of Flowers. Hence my excuse for offering these pages, either to those who may be intending to visit, or to those who may wish to recall the memories of a sojourn in the Land of the Rising Sun.

The book does not pretend to furnish a complete list of all the flowers to be found in the country, but rather to give a description of those which are most remarkable for their beauty and profusion, and which are most closely associated with Japan. The pages on landscape gardening have been condensed, partly owing to want of space, and also because I felt that those who take a real and thorough interest in the subject have Mr. Conder's admirable volumes on "Landscape Gardening in Japan" to help them in the study of the most complicated form of gardening in the world. Being debarred, through lack of sufficient knowledge of the language, from availing myself of original works in Japanese, I have drawn much information from Mr. Conder's works, and from those of other foreigners; but I wish gratefully to acknowledge the help I received from Mr. Y. Noguchi, who provided me with the flower legends and fairy tales, which are household words in every Japanese home.

FLORENCE DU CANE.

CONTENTS

CHAP.		PAGE
1. Landscape Gardening		1
2. Stones—Garden Ornaments and Fences		19
3. Landscape Gardens		38
4. Nursery Gardens—Dwarf Trees and Hachi-niwa		55
5. Temple Gardens		72
6. Summer Flowers		87
7. Plum Blossom		104
8. Peach Blossom		119
9. Cherry Blossom		127
10. Wistaria and Pæony		146
11. Azaleas		161
12. The Iris		169
13. The Morning Glory		181
14. The Lotus		186
15. The Chrysanthemum		197
16. The Maple Leaves		214
17. The Bamboo		223
18. The Pine-Tree		236

LIST OF ILLUSTRATIONS

		FACING PAGE
1. Wistaria, Kyomidzu		*Frontispiece*
2. Wistaria in a Kyoto Garden		4
3. The Storks		12
4. Azaleas in a Kyoto Garden		22
5. Azaleas, Kyoto		28
6. Tiger Lilies		34
7. An Old Garden		40
8. Satake Garden, Tokyo		42
9. A Tokyo Garden		46
10. A Landscape Garden		52
11. The Old Wistaria		60
12. At Kitano Tenjin		72
13. The Drooping Cherry		74
14. A Shrine at Kyomidzu		78
15. White Cherry at Kitano		80
16. Cherry Blossom, Chion-in Temple		84
17. The Kobai Plum Blossom		92
18. *Lilium Auratum*		96
19. Lilies on the Rocks, Atami		98
20. An Hydrangea Bush		100
21. Viewing the Plum Blossoms		104
22. The Gate of the Plum Garden		106

FLOWERS AND GARDENS OF JAPAN

	FACING PAGE
23. The Time of the Plum Blossoms	110
24. Plum Blossom and Lanterns	116
25. Peach Blossom	120
26. The Pagoda, Kyomidzu	126
27. A Buddhist Shrine	130
28. The Feast of the Cherry Blossoms	132
29. The Pink Cherry	138
30. Cherry-tree at Kyomidzu	142
31. Wistaria, Kameido	148
32. Wistaria, Nagaoka	152
33. A Pæony Garden	154
34. Wistaria, Kabata	158
35. Azaleas	162
36. Azaleas, Nagaoka	164
37. Azaleas, Awata	166
38. An Iris Garden	172
39. Irises	178
40. Lotus at Kodaiji	186
41. Lotus at Kyomidzu	188
42. Lotus Flowers	194
43. Chrysanthemums, Kyoto	198
44. A Chrysanthemum Garden	204
45. Chrysanthemums	208
46. The Scarlet Maple	214
47. Viewing the Maples	218
48. Irises, Horikiri	230
49. Pine-tree at Matsushima	238
50. Azalea and Pine-tree	244

FLOWERS & GARDENS OF JAPAN

CHAPTER I

LANDSCAPE GARDENING

IT is safe to assert that no other country has such a distinctive form of landscape gardening as Japan. In English, French, Italian, and Dutch gardens, however original in their way, there are certain things they seem all to possess in common: terraces, which originally belonged to Italian gardens, were soon introduced into France; clipped trees, which were a distinctive feature of Dutch gardens, were copied by the English; the fashion of decorating gardens with flights of stone steps, balustrades, fountains, and statues at one time spread from Italy throughout Europe; and possibly the over-decoration of gardens led to a change in taste in England and a return to a more natural style. The gardens of China and Japan have remained unique; the Eastern style of gardening has never spread to any other country, nor is it ever likely to; for, just as no Western artist will ever paint in the same manner as an Oriental artist because his whole artistic sense is different, so no Western gardener could ever hope to construct a garden representing a portion of the natural scenery of Japan—which is the aim and object of every good Japanese landscape garden, however small—because, however long he might study the original scene, he would never arrive at the Japanese conception of it, or realise what it conveyed to the mind of a Japanese. Their art of gardening was originally borrowed from the Chinese, who appear to have been the first to construct miniature mountains, and to bring water from a distance to feed miniature water-falls and mountain torrents. They even went so far as, in one enclosure, to represent separate scenes for different seasons of the year, and different hours of the day, but to the Japanese belongs the honour of having perfected the art of landscape gardening.

It is not my intention to weary the reader with technical information on the subject, which he will find admirably explained in Mr. Conder's volume on *Landscape Gardening in Japan*, but an outline of some of the theories and rules which guide the Japanese gardener will help us to appreciate his work and give an additional interest to the hours spent in these refreshing retreats from the outer world.

The designer of a good landscape garden has to be guided by many things. A scene must be chosen suited to the size of the ground and the house, and its natural surroundings; and the Japanese garden being above all a spot for secluded leisure and meditation, the temperament, sentiment, and even the occupation of the owner are brought into consideration. Their conception of the expression of nature is governed in its execution by endless æsthetic rules; considerations of scale, proportion, unity, and balance, in fact all that tends to artistic harmony, must be considered, so as to preserve the perfect balance of the picture, and any neglect would destroy that feeling of repose which is so essential in the landscape garden. When we realise that the art has occupied the minds of poets, sages, and philosophers, it is not to be wondered at that something more than the simple representation of natural views has entered into the spirit of their schemes, which attain to poetical conceptions; and a garden may be designed to suggest definite ideas and associations, in fact the whole art is enshrouded by quaint æsthetic principles, and it is difficult for the Western mind to unravel the endless laws and theories by which it is governed.

In gardens which cover a larger area the scheme must necessarily be very different from that required for the making of a tiny garden, only some few yards square, but the materials used will be the same; only the stone bridges and garden ornaments will all be in proportion to the size of the garden, for the rule of proportion is perhaps the most important of all. I visited a garden which was being enlarged by the addition of a hill and the suggestion of mountain forests, to give the impression of unknown limits. The owner explained that as he had enlarged his house it was therefore necessary at the same time to enlarge his garden. A landscape garden may be of any size, from the miniature scenes, representing pigmy groves, and mossy precipices, with lilliputian torrents of white sand, compressed into the area of a china dish, to the vast gardens with their broad sheets of water and majestic trees which surrounded the Daimyo castles of old or the Imperial palaces of to-day; but the sense of true proportion must be rigidly adhered to. Large rocks and boulders are out of

WISTARIA IN A KYOTO GARDEN

LANDSCAPE GARDENING

place in a small garden, and small stones in a large garden would be equally unsuitable. The teachers of the craft have been most careful to preserve the purity of style. Over-decoration is condemned as vulgar ostentation, and faulty designs have even been regarded as unlucky, in order to avoid degeneration in the art.

In some of the most extensive gardens it is not uncommon to represent several favourite views, and yet the composition will be so contrived that all the separate scenes work into one harmonious whole. In the immediate foreground of a nobleman's house there will be an elaborately finished garden full of detail and carefully composed, the stones employed will be the choicest, the water-basin of quaint and beautiful design. Stone lanterns in keeping with the scene will be found, miniature pagodas possibly, and a few slabs of some precious stone to form the bridges. Farther away from the house the scheme should be less finished. Surrounding the simple room set apart for the tea ceremony the law forbids the garden to be finished in style, it must be rather rough and sketchy, and then if some natural wild scene is represented, a broad effect must be retained; a simple clump of pines or cryptomerias near a little garden shrine will represent some favourite temple, or a small grove of maples and cherry-trees by the side of a stream of running water will suggest the scenery of Arashiyama or some other romantic and poetical spot.

To our Western ideas it seems impossible that a garden without flowers could be a thing of beauty, or give any pleasure to its owner. Yet, strange as it may appear, flowers for their own sakes do not enter into the scheme of Japanese gardening, and if any blossoms are to be found, it is probably, so to speak, by accident, because the particular shrub or plant which may happen to be in flower was the one best suited by its growth for the position it occupies in the garden. For instance, azaleas are often seen covering the banks with gorgeous masses of colour, but they are only allowed, either on account of their picturesque growth and the fact that they are included in the natural vegetation of the scene produced, or else because the bushes can be cut into regulation shapes, which, as often as not, is done when the flowers are just opening. Though the Japanese are great lovers of flowers, their taste is so governed by rules, that they are extremely fastidious in their choice of the blossoms they consider worthy of admiration. The rose and the lily are rejected as unworthy, their charms are too obvious: their favourites are the iris, pæony, wistaria, lotus, morning glory, and chrysanthemum; and even among these the iris, wistaria, and possibly the lotus, are the only ones which seem ever to be allowed to belong in any way to the real design of the garden. Flowering trees take more part, and the plum, peach, cherry, magnolia, and camellia are all permitted; and the numerous fancy varieties of the maple, whose leaves enrich the autumn landscape with their scarlet glory, are as much prized as any of the blossoming shrubs. It is rather to the storm-bent old pine-trees and other evergreen trees and shrubs, to the mossy lichen-covered stones, to the clever manipulation of the water to represent a miniature mountain cascade or a flowing river, and to broad stretches of velvety moss that the true Japanese garden owes its beauty.

Mr. Conder tells us that the earliest style of gardening in the country was called the *Imperial Audience Hall Style*, because, not unnaturally, it was round the palaces and houses of the great nobles that the idea was first adopted of arranging the ground to suggest a real landscape. The designs appear to have been primitive, but they usually contained a large irregular lake, with at least one island reached by a bridge of picturesque form. Later—from the middle of the twelfth to the beginning of the fourteenth century—the art of gardening was much practised and encouraged by the Buddhist priests. They even went so far as to ascribe imaginary religious and moral attributes to the grouping of the stones, a custom which has more or less survived to this day and is described elsewhere. In those days a lake came to be regarded as a necessary feature, and poetical names were given to the little islets, just as the pine-clad islands of Matsu-shima have each their poetical name. Cascades also received names according to their character, such as the "Thread Fall," the "Spouting Fall," or the "Side Fall." In the making of a garden then, as to-day, the first work was the excavation of the lake, the designing and forming of the islands, the placing in position of a few of the most important stones, and finally the arrangement of the waterfall or stream which was to feed the lake, and the outlet had also to be carefully considered. After this period came the fashion of representing lakes and rivers by means of hollowed-out beds and courses, merely strewn with sand, pebbles, and boulders, a practice followed also to this day where water is not available. Shallow water or dried-up river-beds are suggested in this way, and therefore the style received the name of *Dried-up Water Scenery*. Artificial hills were used, stones and winding pathways were introduced, and large rocks helped to suggest natural scenery.

It was in the fifteenth century that the art of gardening received the greatest encouragement and attention at the hands of the Ashikaya Regents, who also encouraged the other arts of flower arrangement — tea ceremony and poetry. The Professors of *Cha no yu* (tea ceremony) became the principal designers of gardens, and they naturally turned their attention to the ground which surrounded the rooms set apart for this ceremonial tea-drinking; and to the famous Soami, who was a Professor of Tea-ceremonial and the Floral Art, they owe the practice of clipping trees and shrubs into fantastic shapes. Though the Japanese never attained to the unnatural eccentricities of the Dutch in their manner of using clipped trees, yet in many old and modern gardens a pine-tree may be seen clipped and trained in the shape of a junk, and a juniper may be trained to form a light bridge to fling across a tiny stream; but as a rule the gardener contents himself by training and clipping his pine-tree to mould it into the shape of an abnormal storm-bent specimen of great age. To that period belonged Kobori Enshiu, the designer of so many celebrated gardens, and to him we owe the garden of the Katsura Rikui, a detached Palace near Kyoto, which, though fallen into decay, retains much of its former beauty, especially when the scarlet azalea bushes, which now escape the clipping they no doubt were subjected to in old days, light up the scene, their lichen-clad stems bending under the weight of their blossoms and enhancing the beauty of the moss-grown lanterns and stones. The garden which surrounded the temple of Kodaiji, a portion only of the grounds of the old palace of Awata, the Konchi-in garden of the Nanzenji Temple, and many other specimens of his work remain in Kyoto alone. He is reported to have said that his ideal garden should express "the sweet solitude of a landscape clouded by moonlight, with a half gloom between the trees." Rikiu, another great tea professor and designer of landscape gardens, said the best conception of his fancy would be that of the "lonely precincts of a secluded mountain shrine, with the red leaves of autumn scattered around." However different their ideal, they all agreed that the tea garden was to be somewhat wild in character, suggesting repose and solitude. Then came the more modern style of gardening: from 1789 to 1830 was a period when large palaces were built and surrounded by magnificent gardens, fit residences for the great Tokugawa feudal lords. For these gardens great sums were expended on collecting stones from all parts of the country, and often a garden would be left unfinished until the exact stone suited to express the required religious or poetical feeling, or else specially required to complete a miniature natural scene, had been procured. The extravagance in this craving for rare stones, which cost vast sums to transport immense distances, reached such a pitch, that at last, in the Tempo period (1830-1844), an edict was issued limiting the sum which might be paid for a single specimen. Stone and granite lanterns of infinite variety in size and shape were introduced with their poetical names, each having a special position assigned to it by the unbending laws which surround this art, for the arrangement of not only every tree and stone, but almost every blade of grass and drop of water. I feel my readers will begin to think that there must be a lack of variety in these landscape gardens, but I can safely say that never did I see—and I saw a great many—any two gardens, large or small, which bore any resemblance to each other; the materials are the same, but the design is never the same.

Garden water-basins, miniature pagodas, stone bridges, also of infinite variety, and other garden ornaments, such as rustic arbours, fanciful constructions of bamboo, reeds, or plaited rushes, primitive, fragile-looking structures, but none the less costly, were made use of, and a few rare birds, such as storks and cranes, were allowed to wander and adorn the scene with their stately grace. Here and there the crooked branches of stunted pine-trees of great age overhung the lake or stream, transplanted probably with infinite care; but no trouble and no expense was too great to make these gardens fitting settings for the castles and palaces of those great lords. Alas, how few remain to-day in anything like their former splendour; the hand of the Goth has swept away most of the ancient glories of Yedo, and on the spot where these princely dwellings and gardens stood, to-day some great factory chimneys rise and belch forth columns of smoke, which will surely bring death and destruction to the pines and cherry-trees

THE STORKS

LANDSCAPE GARDENING

of Uyeno or the avenues of Mukojima, which are still the pride of Tokyo.

Tokyo may still retain the remains of some of her princely gardens, but I fear she has lost her love of gardening; the town is too large, too crowded; the rich who could afford to make new gardens, even if the old ones are swept away, prefer to live in foreign houses of impossible architectural design; the public gardens are no longer laid out in true Japanese style, but suggestive rather of foreign gardens of the worst form and taste, so if you would see the making of a new garden it is to Kyoto you must wend your way. Here the love of landscape gardening seems still alive, and though the gardens may not surround the palaces of the Daimyos, yet these humbler gardens which as often as not surround the house of a rich Osaka tradesman are none the less beautiful for that reason; and I was glad to think that riches had not, as is too often the case, brought with it a love for foreign life and stamped out the true Japanese, and that here at least are left many who are content to spend their hours of leisure in the contemplation and in the repose of a true landscape garden.

In the course of an evening walk on the outskirts of Kyoto I came upon a half-built house. Through the newly planted cryptomeria hedge could be seen glimpses of stone lanterns, rocks, and a few trees kept in place by bamboo props, while in the road outside lay stones of all colours, shapes, and sizes. Garden coolies were passing in and out, carrying baskets of earth slung on bamboo poles, so it was evident that a garden was being made. My curiosity was aroused, so I ventured within the enclosure, and, in the most polite language I could command, asked permission of the owner to watch the interesting work. A Japanese is always gratified by the genuine interest of a foreigner in anything connected with his home, and will usually point out the special features of the object of interest in eloquent and poetical phrases, confusing enough to the foreigner, whose command of the Japanese language cannot as a rule rise to such heights. On this occasion, however, any explanation was unnecessary, the scene in itself was sufficient to call forth my admiration and surprise. The piece of ground occupied by the garden did not comprise more than half an acre, and was merely the plot usually attached to any suburban villa in England. Notwithstanding the limited space, a perfect landscape was growing out of the chaos of waste ground which had been chosen as the site of the house. A miniature lake of irregular shape had been dug out; an island consisting of just one bold rock, to be christened no doubt in due time with some fanciful name, had been placed in position; and there were the "Guardian Stone," always the most important stone in the near distance, and its associates the "Stone of Worship"—also sometimes called the "Stone of Contemplation," as from this stone the best general view of the garden is obtained—and the "Stone of the Two Deities." The presence of these three stones being essential in the composition of every garden, they are probably the first to be placed. A few trees of venerable appearance had already been planted in the orthodox places; and already one spreading pine-tree stretched across the future lake, supported on an elaborate framework of bamboo, to give it exactly the right shape and direction; near to it, and resting on a slab of rock at the very edge of the water, was a stone lantern of the "Snow Scene" shape; the two forming the principal features of the garden, upon which the eye rested involuntarily. Another stone lantern stood in the shadow of a tall and twisted pine, half buried in low-growing shrubs, bedded in moss of a golden-brown colour. On one side was a bank thickly planted with azaleas, groups of maples, or camellias, and at the far end of the garden some tall evergreen trees cleverly disguised the boundary line of the hedge and gave the impression that the garden had no ending, save in the wooded hills that shut in the surrounding valley. A cutting in the bank and a wonderfully natural arrangement of "Cascade Stones" showed where the water would eventually rush in from the stream outside, which had its source in Lake Biwa. A path of beaten earth with stepping-stones embedded in it wound round the little lake and through the grove at the side; a simple bridge of mere slabs of stone crossed the water to where the pathway ended in the inevitable tea-room. Many more lanterns, pagodas, and other garden ornaments lay on the ground waiting for their allotted place, while a whole nursery of trees carefully laid in loose earth showed that much more planting was needed to complete the garden, which would some day be the pride and delight of the owner's heart.

The whole country is often searched for a tree of exactly the right size and shape required for a particular position, and while watching the work

LANDSCAPE GARDENING

of making this new garden I was much struck by the extraordinary skill the Japanese display in the transplanting of trees of almost any size and age. The season chosen for their removal is the spring, when the sap is rising, and the dampness of the climate and the rich soil no doubt help considerably towards their success in moving these old trees; unlike England, spring is their best season for planting, as the trees will have all the benefit of the summer rains and run no risk of drought or cold winds. The roots are trenched round, to our idea, perilously near the tree; as much earth is retained as possible and bound round with matting. Five or six coolies with a length of rope, a few poles, and not a little ingenuity, will move the largest tree in a very short time. There is no machinery or fuss of any kind, merely a hand-barrow, on which the tree rests on its journey. Very little preparation is made in the place where the tree is to be planted; no trenching of the ground, or preparing of vast holes to be filled with prepared soil, only a hole just large enough for the ball of earth surrounding the roots is considered sufficient. The tree is then put in place, upright or leaning, according to the effect required, the soil tightly rammed round the roots, the necessary pruning and propping carefully attended to; the ground artistically planted with moss and made to look as if it had never been disturbed for centuries, and the thing is done. I remember seeing a piece of ground which was being prepared for building, on which were a few plum-trees of considerable size and age; these were being carefully removed, doubtless to give a venerable appearance to some new garden, or to be planted in a nursery garden until they should be wanted elsewhere,—surely a better fate than would have awaited them in our country under similar circumstances, where the devastating axe of the builder's labourer would certainly have cleared the ground in a few minutes of what he would have regarded as useless rubbish.

CHAPTER II

STONES—GARDEN ORNAMENTS AND FENCES

Stones and rocks are such important features in all Japanese gardens that when choosing the material for the making of a landscape garden, however large or however small, the selection of the stones would appear to be the primary consideration. Their size must be in perfect proportion with the house and grounds which they are to transform into a natural landscape, and they will give the scale for all the other materials used—the lanterns, bridges, and water-basins, and even the trees and fences. Their number may vary from five important stones to as many as 138, each with its especial sense and function. I think the correct position and placing of the stones is the part of the art which it would be most difficult for a foreigner to accomplish: the mere names and special functions of the stones would require years of careful study.

To the eye of a Japanese one stone wrongly placed would upset all the balance and repose of the picture. Large rocks and boulders seem to be essential for the success of a large garden, and are used to suggest mountains, hills, and the rocks of the natural scene; any very fantastic and artificial-looking rocks are avoided, for fear they should give an appearance of unreality to the landscape. The fancy of giving sex to certain stones, and in temple grounds of assigning holy attributes and even of giving them the names of Buddhist deities, dates from very early days, and this custom of applying a religious meaning to the most important rocks survives to this day. Mr. Conder tells us that "formerly it was said that the principal boulders of a garden should represent the *Kuji*, or Nine Spirits of the Buddhist pantheon, five being of *standing* and four of *recumbent* form; and it was supposed that misfortune was averted by observing this classification." Stones of good shape, colour, and proportion are treasured as carefully as any jewel, and in the gardens of the rich are brought together from all parts of the empire. The granite for slabs, steps, and lanterns may come from the neighbourhood of Osaka, Bingo, and other places. Large blocks which have an irregular surface are usually limestones, and the action of water has produced those much coveted shapes. Blue and white limestone and a kind of jasper rock of a reddish colour are prized for certain positions, slabs of a dark green colour seemed to come from the vicinity of Lake Biwa, and volcanic rock and honeycombed sea-rocks are valuable for water scenes. It would only weary the reader if I were to attempt to describe the endless combinations of stones as laid down by the unbending laws, or to give all the names applied to the various sets of stones known as Hill Stones, Lake and River Stones, Cascade Stones, Island Stones, Valley Stones, Water-basin Stones, Tea-garden Stones, and, finally, Stepping-Stones. Often did I regret that my knowledge of the art was not sufficient to enable me to recognise all these various stones. How intensely it would add to one's appreciation of these perfect specimens of artificial scenery if one could at once among the *Hill Stones* point out the " Mountain Summit Stone" and the poetical " Propitious Cloud Stone," or the "Mist-enveloped Stone"; or among the *River and Lake Stones* find the "Sentinel Stone," which, as its name suggests, should be placed in the position of a look-out man near the edge of the water; or the "Wave-receiving Stone" hidden in the current

of the stream. So often the water scenery of
the garden is intended to represent sea-views, the
favourite being a portion of the scenery of Matsu-
shima with its countless islets, that many of these
Lake Stones have names suggestive of the sea;
such as the "Sea-gull Resting Stone," situated
on a stony beach, or the "Wild Wave Stone,"
placed so as to meet the current of the water.

Next come the *Cascade Stones*, which do
not seem quite so numerous, and among them
one at least forms so important a feature in
every garden that it is easy to distinguish—the
"Guardian Stone," which should form the main
part of the rocky cliff over which the water falls; it
is also sometimes called the "Cascade-supporting
Stone." "The Stone of Fudo," named after a
Buddhist god, and its eight small attendants, the
"Children Stones," are among the more important
features of the cascade or waterfall.

The *Island Stones* are perhaps more interesting
still, as they are such important features in the landscape. The "Elysian Isle," the "Master's Isle,"
and the "Guest's Isle" are the most favourite trio
of islands, and are formed of combinations of stones.
That of the "Elysian Isle," whose origin comes from
China, is a combination of four stones suggesting

AZALEAS IN A KYOTO GARDEN

the different members of a tortoise's body, and a pine-tree of carefully trained form should grow, as it were, out of the back of the animal. The "Master's Isle" has three principal stones —the "Stone of Easy Rest," which speaks for itself; the "Stone of Amusement," suggesting the best spot for fishing; and finally the "Seat Stone." The "Guest's Isle" has five important stones— the "Guest-honouring Stone"; the "Interviewing Stone"; "Shoe-removing Stone," on which the clogs or sandals are changed; the "Water-fowl Stone"; and again the "Sea-gull Resting Stone."

Among the *Valley Stones* many have a religious suggestion; but under this head we find the important "Stone of Worship," a broad flat stone upon which one has to assume an attitude of veneration; it should be in front of the garden, at the point from which the best view is obtained. The *Water-basin Stones* are not those which form the basin itself, but may merely serve as a base for the actual water receptacle, and either act as an embellishment, or perform certain functions in connection with the basin. The *Tea-garden Stones* have the "Kettle Stone," the "Candlestick Stone," and many others suggestive of the tea-drinking ceremonies—merely fanciful in their names, as these ceremonies invariably take place in a room, and therefore the stones are never used to fulfil their supposed functions.

Finally we come to the *Stepping-Stones*, and the art of the Japanese in placing these stones cannot fail to strike any one who has any interest in the making of an ordinary rock garden. Their presence in all gardens in Japan is essential, as the use of turf being almost, if not entirely, unknown for paths and open spaces, it is replaced by firmly beaten earth, or, for larger spaces, by fine sand carefully raked into patterns; as footmarks, and more especially the marks of wooden clogs, would destroy the symmetry of these patterns, and in damp weather cut up the beaten earth, the use of stones for crossing the spaces or taking a walk round the garden is an absolute necessity. The alternative name for these stones is *Flying Stones* or *Scattered Islands*, which at once suggests how gracefully and artistically they are placed. Nothing, as a rule, could be less artistic than the way stepping-stones are placed in English gardens; they seem at once to bring to my mind visions of people trying to keep a steady gait, a feat which it is positively difficult to accomplish where the stones are laid in an

STONES—ORNAMENTS AND FENCES

almost straight row. In commenting on this fact Mr. Conder says:—

It is not, therefore, surprising to find that the Japanese gardener follows carefully devised rules for the distribution of "Stepping-Stones." He uses certain special stones and combinations, having definite shapes and approximate dimensions assigned to them, and he connects these with secondary blocks, the whole being arranged with a studied irregularity, both for comfort in walking and artistic grace. This is attained by the employment of ragged slabs of slate, schist, or flint, flat water-worn rocks or boulders, and hewn slabs or discs of granite or some other hard stone. The natural boulders are placed in zigzags of fours and threes, or sometimes in threes and twos, artificially hewn slabs, discs, or strips intervening. Though uniformity of tread is carefully calculated, the different sizes of the stones cause the intervals to vary considerably, and any apparent regularity is avoided. The distance between "Stepping-Stones" should not, however, be less than four inches, to allow of the intermediate spaces being kept clean. The smaller stones are of sufficient size for the foot to rest firmly upon, and should not, as a general rule, be higher than two inches from the soil. In ancient times it is said that "Stepping-Stones" for the Emperor's gardens were made six inches high, those for a Daimyo four inches, those for ordinary Samurai nearly three inches, and for common folk an inch and a half in height. The larger stones are intended as a rest for both feet, and two of them should never be used consecutively. In some cases several continuous pathways formed of "Stepping-Stones" may be seen. When such walks branch off in two directions a larger and higher stone, called the "Step-dividing Stone," will be placed at the point of divergence.

The stones leading to the house end usually in a high slab of granite which forms the step on to the verandah. It is no exaggeration to say that the Stepping-Stones of a well-planned garden, besides being of strict utility, are a great ornament to the garden.

Probably the garden ornaments which will first attract the eye of the visitor are the stone lanterns, which are to be found in almost every garden, however humble. These lanterns appear to be of purely Japanese origin; no record of them is to be found in the history of Chinese gardens, though the introduction of miniature stone pagodas as garden ornaments came to Japan from China through the medium of Korea, for which reason they are still called "Korean Towers." The use of stone lanterns as a decoration for gardens seems to date from the days when the Professors of Tea-ceremonial turned their attention to landscape gardening. The custom of presenting votive offerings of lanterns in bronze or stone, large or small, plain or decorated, dates from early days, and no Buddhist temple or shrine is complete without its moss-grown lanterns adorning the courts and grounds. The correct placing of stone lanterns in the landscape garden is almost as complex as the placing of stones. They should be used in combination with rocks, shrubs and trees, and water-basins. They have no use except as ornaments, as seldom, if ever, did I see one with a light in its fire-box except in temple grounds. They appeared to be almost more valued for their age than their form, as new ones can be easily procured of any desired shape; but however ingenious the devices may be for imparting a look of age to new specimens, it is time, and time alone, which will bring that thick green canopy of velvet moss on their roof, and the granite will only become toned down to the coveted mellow hue by long exposure to the weather.

Roughly speaking, garden lanterns are divided into two classes, the *Standard* and the *Legged* class, though many others of fanciful design may sometimes be seen. The origin of the Standard class was known as the "Kasuga" shape, after a Shinto god to whom the well-known Nara temple is dedicated. Thousands of these Kasuga lanterns adorn the temple grounds, and the exact form is that of "a high cylindrical standard, with a small amulet in the centre, erected on a base and plinth of hexagonal plan, and supporting an hexagonal head crowned with a stone roof of double curve, having corner scrolls. The top is surmounted with a ball drawn to a point above. The head of the lantern, which is technically called the fire-box, is hollowed out, two of its faces having a square opening large enough to admit an oil lamp; and the remaining four sides being carved respectively with representations of a stag, a doe, the sun, and the moon." These lanterns may vary in size, from six to as much as eighteen feet, and in this colossal size make a most imposing decoration for a large garden. There are several other designs which closely resemble the true Kasuga shape. Many others there are which still belong to the Standard class: some with the standards shortened and the heads elongated; others with flat saucer-shaped caps or wide mushroom-shaped roofs—in fact, an infinite variety; and even in humble gardens rude specimens are seen built of natural mossy stones chosen to resemble as closely as possible the regulation form, and the fire-box made of wood. Another form of the Standard shape is suggestive of glorified lamp-posts; these lanterns are mostly used in the approach to gardens or near the tea-rooms. Some of them are very quaint and quite rustic in appearance, being always made of wood. The square wooden lantern on a tall post is covered by either a wooden or thatched roof with wide-

AZALEAS, KYOTO

projecting eaves. One of these is called the *Who goes there?* shape, and derives its original name from the fact that the dim light seen through its paper doors is only sufficient to enable a person to vaguely distinguish an approaching form; and the *Thatched Hut* shape is in the form of a little thatched cottage.

The class known as *Legged* lanterns have the alternative name of *Snow Scene* lanterns, as the very wide umbrella-shaped roof or cap, by which they are invariably covered, makes a broad surface for snow to rest upon. To the eye of a Japanese the effect of snow is almost more beautiful than any of their floral displays, and a snow-clad scene gives them infinite pleasure. The position of these lanterns in the garden should be partly overshadowed by the crooked branch of a spreading pine-tree, and certainly after a fall of snow the effect is one of great beauty.

Ornamental bronze or iron lanterns are hung by a chain from the eaves of the verandah of either the principal house or tea-room, and, like the water-basin, are often very beautiful in design. Bronze *Standard* lanterns are never seen in landscape gardens, only as votive offerings to temples; but occasionally an iron lantern with no standard, only resting on low feet, may be placed on a flat stone near the water's edge, or nestling in the shadow of a group of evergreen shrubs. Near the larger Kasuga-shaped lanterns a stepping-stone (or even two, if the lantern be unusually large) should be placed higher than the surrounding ones; these are called *Lamp-lighting Stones*, as by their aid the fire-box can be conveniently reached for lighting the lamp.

A garden water-basin may be either ornamental in form, or merely a very plain hollowed-out stone with a strictly utilitarian aspect. Its position in the garden is invariably the same, within easy reach of the verandah, so that the water can be reached by the wooden ladle which is left by the side of the basin; and usually an ornamental fence of bamboo or rush-work separates it from that part of the house in its immediate neighbourhood. For a small residence, and where the basin is for practical use, the distance from the edge of the verandah should not be more than eighteen inches, and the height three to four feet; but as the law of proportion applies to the water-basin just as it applies to the rest of the composition, the ornamental basin in front of a large house will have to be three or four feet away, and its height seven or eight feet

STONES—ORNAMENTS AND FENCES

from the ground. In this case, in spite of the stepping-stones, the basin becomes merely an ornament, as it is out of reach for practical purposes, and even has to be protected by a separate decorative roof to keep off the rain.

Each shape of basin has its own name, but perhaps one of the most popular forms is that of a natural rock of some unusual shape, hollowed at the top and covered with a delicate little wooden construction, like a tiny shed or temple, to keep the water cool and unpolluted. The *Running-water Basins*, as their name suggests, receive a stream of clear water by means of a little bamboo aqueduct, and in that case arrangement has to be made for the overflow of the water.

As water is so essential in the composition of all landscape gardens, it is not surprising to find that the various styles of bridges which are employed to cross the lake or miniature torrents, and connect the tiny islands with the shore, are so graceful in design, and yet so simple, that they must certainly be classed as ornaments to the garden. The more elaborate bridges of stone or wood are only seen in large gardens. The semicircular arched bridge, of which the best-known example is in the grounds of the Kameido temple in Tokyo, where it forms a most picturesque object in connection with the wistaria-clad trellises, is of Chinese origin, and is supposed to suggest a full moon, as the reflection in the water below completes the circle. It was not these elaborate bridges that I admired most, but rather the simpler forms made out of a single slab of granite slightly carved, spanning a narrow channel, or, more imposing still, two large parallel blocks, overlapping in the middle of the stream, supported by a rock or by a wooden support.

Very attractive, too, are the little bridges made of bundles of faggots laid on a wooden framework, covered with beaten earth, the edges formed of turf, bound with split bamboo, to prevent the soil from crumbling away. There is an infinite variety of these little fantastic bridges, and the cleverness displayed in the placing of them was a never-failing source of admiration to me. The common idea of a bridge being a means of crossing water in the shortest and most direct manner is by no means the Japanese conception of a bridge. Their fondness for water, and their love of lingering while crossing it, in order to feed and gaze at the goldfish, or merely to enjoy the scene, has no doubt been responsible for the position of many of their bridges: one slab will connect the shore with a little rocky islet, and then, instead of continuing in the most direct route to the opposite shore, as often as not the next slab will branch away in an entirely different direction, probably with the object of revealing a different view of the garden, or merely in order to prolong the pleasure of crossing the lake or stream.

In most gardens, unless they are very diminutive in size, there is at least one Arbour or *Resting Shed*. It may consist merely of a thick rustic post supporting a thatched roof in the shape of a huge umbrella, with a few movable seats, or its proportions may assume those of a miniature house carefully finished in every detail. When they are of such an elaborate form they partake more of the nature of the Tea-ceremony room, with raised matted floors, plastered walls, and *shoji* on at least two sides of the room. The open structures in various shapes, with rustic thatched roofs, some fixed seats with a low railing or balustrade to lean against, are of more common form; and if the *Resting House* is by the side of the lake, a projecting verandah railed round is very popular, affording a comfortable resting-place from which to gaze at the scene.

Decorative garden wells are picturesque objects,

with their diminutive roofs to protect the cord and pulley from the rain. As often as not they are purely for ornament, but even in this case the cord, pulley, and bracket should all look as antique as possible. A few stepping-stones should lead to it, and a stone lantern should be at hand with a suitable group of trees or shrubs.

Finally we come to garden fences and gateways, which again are bewildering in their infinite variety and style. The Imperial gardens, and even less imposing domains, are not enclosed by fences, but by solid walls of clay and mud, plastered over, carrying a roof of ornamental tiles. Even fences made of natural wood all carry a projecting roof to afford protection from the rain, which adds very much to their picturesque effect. The humblest garden must have two entrances, which therefore necessitates two gateways—the principal entrance, by which the guests enter, and the back entrance, called *The Sweeping Opening* from its practical use as a means of egress for the rubbish of the garden. This gate will be made of wood or bamboo, quite simple in style; but the *Entrance Gate* is a far more important feature of the domain, and must be in character with the garden it leads to. The actual garden doors are of

TIGER LILIES

natural wood, their panels decorated with either carving or lattice-work, and set in a wooden frame which may vary considerably in style. Roofed gateways are very common, and the practice of hanging a wooden tablet between the lintels, with an inscription either describing the style of the garden or merely conveying a pretty sentiment in keeping with its character, is often seen. The fashion of planting a pine-tree of twisted and crooked shape just inside the gateway so that its leaning branches may be seen above the fence, is not only for artistic effect, but, the pine being an emblem of good luck, it is supposed to bring long life and happiness to the owner of the garden.

Mr. Conder tells us that over a hundred drawings exist of ornamental *Screen Fences*, called by the Japanese *Sleeve Fences*. They may be used to screen off some portion of the garden, but are mainly ornamental, and are usually placed near the water-basin and a stone lantern. Without illustrations it is hopeless to attempt to describe their fanciful shapes, each again with a poetical name. The materials used in their construction consist chiefly of bamboo tubes of various sizes, rushes and reeds tied with dyed fibre, or even the tendrils of creepers or wistaria. In some of the simpler forms the patterns are only made by the placing of the bamboo joints; but others are much more elaborate, and have panels of lattice-work formed of tied rushes or reeds, or openings of different shapes like windows. Mr. Conder gives a detailed description of an immense number of these fantastic screens, and one at least I must quote as an example.

> The *Moon-entering Screen Fence* is about seven feet high and three feet wide, having in the centre a circular hole, from which it receives its name. The vertical border on one side is broken off at the edge of the orifice, so that the circle is not complete, and this gives it the form of a three-quarter moon. Above the hole the bundles of reeds are arranged vertically, like bars, and below in a diagonal lattice-work, tied with hemp cords.

Through the openings in these fences a branch of pine, or some creeper, is often brought through and trained with excellent effect.

I feel I have said enough about the materials used for the construction of a landscape garden, to convey to the mind of the reader something of the difficulties which surround the correct combination of these materials, and sufficient to make any one realise that the making of a Japanese garden is a true art, which it is not surprising that it is impossible for a foreigner to imitate, hence the lamentable failure of the so-called "Japanese gardens" which it has been the fashion of late years to try and make in England frequently by persons who have never even seen one of the gardens of Japan. The owner of probably the best of these English "Japanese gardens" was showing his garden, which was the apple of his eye, to a Japanese, who with instinctive politeness was full of admiration, but had failed to recognise the fact that it was meant to be a true landscape garden of his own country, and therefore exclaimed, "It is very beautiful; we have nothing at all like it in Japan!"

CHAPTER III

LANDSCAPE GARDENS

HAVING made some attempt to elucidate the mysterious and wonderful construction of Japanese gardens, I feel the reader will expect to learn something of their effect as a whole when completed. Unfortunately many of the finest specimens of landscape gardens, the old Daimyos' gardens in Tokyo, have been swept away to make room for foreign houses, factories, and breweries, and no trace of them remains; old drawings or photographs alone tell of their departed glories. Probably the largest of these gardens which still remains entire is the Koraku-en, or Arsenal Garden, as it is more commonly called. It is now empty and deserted, and seems only filled with sadness, its groves recalling days gone by, when succeeding Daimyos entertained their friends in regal pomp, and the sound of revelry broke the silence of the woods;

to-day only the incessant sound of metal hammering metal breaks the silence of the glades, and the sound of explosions from the Arsenal near by might well rouse the dead. The garden covers a large extent of ground, and is an example of a scheme in which many separate scenes were skilfully worked together to form a perfect whole. Its fame dates from early in the seventeenth century, when the Daimyo of Mito, who was a great patron of landscape gardening, laid out the grounds. The fact that they are remarkable for many Chinese characteristics is not surprising, when we learn that the Shogun Iyemitsu took an interest in the work, and lent the aid of a great Chinese artist called Shunseu, who completed the scheme. A semi-circular stone bridge of Chinese design, called a *Full-moon Bridge*, spans a stretch of water in which, in the scorching heat of August mornings, the great buds of white lotus flowers will crack and slowly open, their giant leaves almost hiding the bridge; this important feature of the garden is called Seiko Kutsumi, after a famous lotus lake in China. The island in the lake is the Elysian Isle of Chinese fame, and formerly was connected with the shore by a long wooden bridge, which has long since disappeared; but the path wanders on, past the rocky shore, skirting the headland and high wooded promontory, through the dense gloom of a forest, and by the time I had made a complete tour of this garden I felt as though I had paid a flying visit to half Japan.

There was an avenue of cherry-trees to recall the avenues of Koganei; the river Tatsuda in miniature, its banks clothed with maples and other reddening trees, to give colour to the garden in autumn, when the setting sun will seem to light the torch and set all the trees ablaze; there also is the Oi-gawa or Rapid River with its wide pebble-strewn bed, down which a rapid-flowing stream is brought; then we are transported to scenes in China; and beyond, again, the wanderer is reminded of the scenery of Yatsuhashi, where one of the eight bridges crosses in zigzag fashion a marshy swamp which in the month of June is a mass of irises, great gorgeous blossoms of every conceivable shade of lilac and purple, completely hiding their foliage; then this little valley becomes a stream of colour and recalls the more extensive glories of Hori-kiri.

Perhaps most ingenious of all is that part of the garden where the cone of Fuji-yama appears, snow-capped in May, as it is densely planted with

AN OLD GARDEN

white azaleas. Many other scenes there were—tiny shrines built in imitation of great temples, cascades and waterfalls named after other celebrated falls, rare rocks, moss-grown lanterns, bridges of all designs; in fact, the garden seemed a perfect treasure-house, and I felt glad that this one garden has escaped the hand of the destroyer and is left entire, a masterpiece of conception and execution.

Of another Tokyō garden—which unfortunately has not been left untouched, as it is shorn of half its former glories, a glaring red-brick brewery covering half the area of the beautiful grounds formerly known as Satake-no-niwa—only a portion remains, though a very lovely portion, and as it seems complete in itself it is still worth a visit. Unlike the Koraku-en, the Satake Garden was a rather artificial example of hill gardening, more open, with no dense groves, but essentially a hill and water garden. The large lake remains, and, like most of the gardens in the Honjo district of Tokyo, its waters are salt and tidal, being connected with the neighbouring river Sumida. Thus at high and low tide the shores of the lake present a very different aspect; pebbly bays can only be crossed by stepping-stones at high tide, and even some of the stone lanterns by the water's edge have their standards half submerged. The hills are closely planted with evergreen bushes and shrubs, and most of the year the garden is all grey and green; the island is reached by a grey stone bridge formed of two slabs of granite of giant proportions, the grey lanterns stand among shrubs, cut into rounded form, and the mossy rocks and boulders have still more neutral tones; so it is only in spring when Nature asserts herself, and no gardener can prevent the young leaves of the maples being a variety of vivid colouring, and the grey rounded azalea bushes become perfect balls of scarlet, rosy-pink and white blossoms, that the garden has any colour in it. But to the mind of the Japanese all sense of repose and quiet charm would be gone if the eye were always worried by a distracting mass of colour; so even if flowers were grown in these more extensive gardens they had a special part of the grounds set apart for their culture. In one corner of the lake a piece of swampy ground was thickly planted with irises and water-plants, and a wistaria trellis overhung the lake, otherwise no flowers entered into the scheme; but it was a perfect specimen of the typical Japanese arrangement of garden hills planted with rounded bushes and adorned with lanterns.

SATAKE GARDEN, TOKYO

LANDSCAPE GARDENS

A magnificent example of a modern landscape garden is that belonging to Baron Iwasaki, made some forty years ago. The venerable pine-trees supported by stout props overhanging the lake are suggestive of countless ages; but in this garden old trees of gnarled and twisted growth, rare rocks, and immense boulders were collected from all parts of the empire, regardless of expense, and brought together to ensure the success of the scheme. The grounds cover many acres, the one blot in the landscape being the large red-brick foreign house; but luckily the most lovely part of the garden is laid out in front of the perfect specimen of a Japanese gentleman's house, where the verandah of the cool matted rooms looks over a scene of indescribable beauty. The large lake is cleverly divided, and the portion of the garden in front of the foreign house is left behind; groves of evergreen trees screen the house—the one jarring note; and here the lake becomes the lagoon of Matsu-shima, tiny pine-clad islets rise from the water, and in the distance rises the cone of Fuji from an undulating plain of close-mown turf and groups of dwarfed pines. Here again flowers have no official existence; azaleas there are in profusion, but they are only introduced as shrubs; so the garden is not a flower garden, but a true landscape garden—the reproduction in miniature of natural scenery. The lanterns and bridges near the foreign house are of immense size, carrying out the law of proportion; the rocks and boulders are large to correspond, and the whole effect is one of great breadth; only near the tea-house and the main Japanese house does the garden become more finished in style and on a smaller scale. The balcony overhangs the rocky edge of the tidal lake; each rock has its history and its especial place; but the laws which have governed the making of such a garden are laws drawn up by great artists,—there is no false note, even the grouping of the reeds and irises by the water's edge has been planned by a master hand, so the picture remains graven on one's memory as that of an ideal pleasaunce for leisure and repose.

In Kyoto there still remain the gardens of the Gold and Silver Pavilions—gardens of much older date, the splendour of their pavilions dimmed by age, more especially in the case of Kinkakuji, the Golden Pavilion. Mr. Conder says, "Long neglect has converted what was once an elaborate artificial landscape into a wild natural scene of great beauty." The little pine-clad islets remain, but they are now island wildernesses; the trees have partially resumed their normal shapes; great leaning pines overhang the shores of the *Mirror Ocean*, representing the Sea of Japan, and its three islands suggesting the Empire of the Mikado. It was in the fourteenth century that this quiet spot became the so-called retreat of the scheming Yoshimitsu, who, pretending to have resigned the Shogunate in favour of his son, here lived in the garb of a monk, but in reality directing the affairs of State. The two-storied Pavilion itself, seen reflected in the *Mirror Ocean*, is possibly more picturesque in decay than it was in the days of its splendour; the gilding from which it takes its name has been partially restored; it is backed by the wooded hill fancifully called the *Silken Canopy* or *Silk Hat Mountain*, from the fact that the ex-Mikado Uda ordered it to be covered with white silk on a scorching summer's day, in order that his eyes might enjoy the sensation of gazing on a cool, snow-covered scene. To this day the garden of Kinkakuji under a light canopy of snow is one of the favourite sights of the people of Kyoto. In days gone by there were smaller arbours in which the Shogun, wearied with his walk among the groves of the *Silk Hat*

Mountain, would rest, and compare the scene which the garden was intended to represent, to the real Sea of Japan, whence the name of one of the arbours, *The House of the Sound of the Seashore*.

To the north-east of Kyoto, nestling among the woods that clothe the lower hills of Hiei-san, lie the grounds of Ginkakuji or the Silver Pavilion. In imitation of his predecessor Yoshimitsu, the Shogun Yoshimasa after his abdication retired from the affairs of the world, built himself a country house with grounds of vast extent, even with despotic impatience sweeping away a temple because it interfered with his plans,—though we are told he was filled with remorse, and afterwards restored it at great expense. The two-storied Pavilion was partly copied from its rival, the Golden Pavilion, though it never seems to have attained to the same splendour; but here the ex-Shogun and his boon companions, the philosopher Soami and Shuko the Nara priest, held their æsthetic revels. They may be said to have laid down the laws which raised the tea-ceremonial to the rank of a fine art. Mr. Farrar, in writing of it, says:—

It has its prescribed ritual of appalling rigidity, this tea-ceremony, invented and elaborated by a pious monk to

A TOKYO GARDEN

LANDSCAPE GARDENS

distract a young and giddy Shogun from his debaucheries. It was taken up as a political weapon by the House of Tokugawa, and crystallised into its present adamantine form, becoming a social engine of the most powerful nature in its power of bringing all the nobles together. Here, then, is one of its temples where the rites were celebrated in their due ordinance, with their prescribed compliments, obeisances, and admiring exclamations over the prescribed flower, arranged in the prescribed spot, and indicated by the host in the prescribed words, to be followed by the invariable litany of conversation and courtesy over the cup of tea to be made, handed, accepted, and drunk all with remarks and gestures and smiles of ancestral rubric.

Outside any tea-house built in accordance with these prescribed regulations one sees "a row of stepping-stones, finishing beneath a little *œil-de-bœuf* in the wall above, by which the visitors had to enter, ignoring the thoroughly practical door. They approached, making the due bows upon each stone, and at last their host was to fish them in through the window."

Another ceremony inaugurated within these precincts was the ceremonial of "incense sniffing," to our minds merely an innocent, childish game, the winner being the person possessing the keenest sense of smell, as the pastime consisted of five or more different kinds of incense being burnt, sniffed, given poetical names, then mixed up and sniffed again, and the man who guesses best the names of the various kinds, is the winner. The boxes which contained the incense, the burners in which it was burnt, were all works of art, and the same grave etiquette which governed the tea-ceremonial governed these incense-sniffing parties, in which poets, writers, priests, philosophers, Daimyos, Shoguns, the greatest and most learned in the land, took part. We can only gaze with wonder and perplexity—not hoping to understand—at a "nation's intellect going off on such devious tracks as this incense-sniffing and the still more intricate tea-ceremonies, and on bouquets arranged philosophically, and gardens representing the cardinal virtues. Such strict rules, such grave faces, such endless terminologies, so much ado about nothing!" (Professor Chamberlain's *Things Japanese.*)

To return to the garden proper, laid out with great elaboration by Soami. Although it is now much neglected, the trees are not kept trimmed according to the rigid laws, their stems are lichen-clad, and Nature has tried to reassert herself over art, yet the beauty of the spot is great. The lake, of ingenious form, backed on the north side by the thickly pine-clad hills and to the west by the regulation grove of maples, is an admirable example of the arrangement of garden stones, its shores being rich in rare and precious rocks, each with its characteristic name. One of the principal stones lying in the lake is the stone of *Ecstatic Contemplation*; the little bridge which divides the lake is the *Bridge of the Pillar of the Immortals*; the water of the cascade which fills the lake, being of exceptional purity, is called the *Moon-washing Fountain*. In the foreground of many of these older gardens was an open space covered with white sand, carefully raked into ornamental patterns, and here is a large mound of the sand suggestive of a mammoth sugar-loaf with a flattened top, called the *Silver Sand Platform*, the smaller one of the same shape being the *Mound facing the Moon*; on these sat Yoshimasa and his favourites, indulging in another favourite pastime of moon-gazing, to our prosaic minds merely another elaborately conceived method of killing time. I know no garden in Japan which seemed to take one back so far into the world of the Old Japan as this little garden of Ginkakuji, and no more peaceful spot to sit and enjoy the reddening maple leaves on a bright evening in late autumn, when there is a touch of sadness in the air, in keeping with the departed glories of the Pavilion and the fast-fading beauties of the trees.

Many of the smaller and most interesting gardens in Japan are those attached to tea-houses or small suburban houses, showing, as they do, the ingenuity and resource of the landscape gardener in making a perfect garden of any size, from ten acres to half an acre, or only a few square yards. Among tea-house gardens, that attached to the Raku-raku-tei at Hikone can hardly be counted, as it was formerly the garden of a great Daimyo and is one of the finest gardens in the country. The numerous little summer-houses built out on piles in the lake have been erected for the entertainment of the guests of the tea-house, a gathering place for the most *élite*, but otherwise the garden remains unchanged; the paths which wind round the lake, across the bridges, past the *Stone of Worship*, from where the beauties of the garden may be enjoyed to best advantage, are the same paths which the feet of successive Daimyos trod in the feudal days of old.

It is rather to the Hira-niwa, or Flat Gardens, that I allude, made in the small enclosures at the back of private houses or tea-houses in towns, or even in the actual courts, no space being apparently too small for the construction of one of these little fresh-looking and artistic gardens. How superior to the dusty, neglected back garden or court of a European house, too often only a piece of waste ground where the rubbish of the house accumulates, the space being condemned as too small for a garden. I can recall visions of many a tiny court no more than twenty feet square, within whose limits were compressed a liliputian pond, fed with clear water by the overflow of the water-basin; a dwarf pine, the soul of every Japanese garden, which in conjunction with a few small evergreen shrubs sheltered a moss-grown lantern. Some small rocks and a few foliage or water plants in a tuft by the water's edge, were the sole materials used for the making of this court-garden. Stepping-stones, let into the beaten earth, led from the step of the verandah to the edge of the pond, ending in one stone larger than the rest, suggesting the *Stone of Worship*, or the *Stone of Amusement*, in case there should be any goldfish in the pond. As these little courts are kept profusely watered, being sprinkled out of a wooden ladle several times a day in the hottest days of summer, the effect is always damp and cool, the mossy stones are always fresh and green, however fierce the heat may be. The variety in the actual form of these gardens seemed infinite; in some the pond was omitted, and the suggestion of water and dampness came from the rustic garden well or the ornamental water-basin, behind which always stands a portion of screen-fencing of elaborate design. When the area is not quite so limited, bridges will be introduced to cross the pond, possibly consisting only of a single stone slab supported on a natural piece of rock, or a granite bridge slightly curved in form, or perhaps only the suggestion of a bridge, formed of a branch of juniper or some flat close-growing evergreen trained in a curve across the water. According to the size of the ground, so these gardens will increase in elaboration of their design, and many an enclosure at the back of a merchant's house in Kyoto or Osaka has been transformed into a perfect specimen of Hira-niwa.

One I recall which always gave me as much pleasure as the most extensive landscape garden in the country. The lake was of the prescribed form known as the *Running Water shape*, fed by a fast-flowing stream which came in at the far end of the garden over the regulation Cascade Stones; a garden arbour of elaborate form overlooked the lake, in which stood the "Elysian Isle" with its pine-tree

A LANDSCAPE GARDEN

growing out of the rock, and a few azalea bushes filling the interstices of the stone, forming a most attractive feature of the garden; banks there were planted with more azaleas; pines, kept dwarfed to about two feet in height, grew out of cushions of thick moss; bridges crossed and re-crossed the stream; stepping-stones, discs, and label stones guided our feet as we wandered about at leisure. There were the two garden entrances, and even the back entrance, or *Sweeping Opening*, was a thing of beauty. Every detail of this garden had been first carefully thought out, and then as carefully carried into execution.

The landscape gardener in Japan is no gardener in the sense that we regard a gardener in the West —a cultivator of flowers: he is a garden artist; he leaves none of his effects to chance; so carefully are his plans made that before the first sod of the new garden has been turned, he knows exactly how the garden will look when completed. He will see in his mind's eye the appointed place for every tree, every stone, which is to be used in its composition. I could not help thinking that if more thought were given to the planning of our English gardens there might be something more complete and satisfying to the eye than the meaningless gardens—often laid out by the owner of the house, who by the wildest stretch of imagination could not be called a garden artist—which too often surround our English homes. Our gardens are made beautiful in summer by the wealth and profusion of their flowers; but when the winter comes and the beds are shorn of their summer glories, the deficiencies of the plan of the garden are laid bare, and might well give us food for thought through the long winter months.

CHAPTER IV

NURSERY GARDENS—DWARF TREES AND HACHI-NIWA

A NURSERY garden in Japan may be called a revelation in the art of pruning. A singular idea exists in the minds of many people, that all the trees in Japan are like the dwarf specimens they have occasionally seen in England on a nurseryman's stand at a flower-show, and frequently they display surprise, not unmixed with incredulity, when assured that such is not the case. I would recommend those unbelievers to take a walk in the cryptomeria avenues at Nikko, among the camphor groves of Atami, or to wander through the pine-woods which clothe the hillsides above Kyoto, when they would see for themselves the magnificence of the trees, untouched by the pruning knife of the gardener. The Japanese bestow as much time and care on the trees in their gardens as the

Western gardener would give to his choicest flowers. The gardener's ideal tree is not the ordinary tree of the forest, but the abnormal specimen which age and weather have twisted and bent into quaint and unusual shapes. Here, in the nursery garden, we shall find specimen trees; old trees it is true, but trees giving proof that art has had to improve upon nature, as scarcely a single tree in the whole collection—waiting, possibly, to transform the new garden of a *nouveau riche* into an ancestral home—will have been allowed to follow its own inclination of growth and shape.

The pine-tree is generally chosen as the subject for the operating knife, and is cut and trained into all manner of shapes; an umbrella made of a single tree of *Pinus densiflora* trained on a framework of light bamboo, or a junk of perfect form, the reward of years of patience, will be waiting until it is required to be the chief feature in a landscape garden. The curiously twisted appearance characteristic of a Japanese pine-tree, in gardens and temple grounds, is achieved by a clever system of pruning, and gives the trees a stunted and venerable appearance, which they would otherwise not attain for years. The leading shoot of each branch and most of the side ones are removed, giving the branch

NURSERY GARDENS

a new direction, sometimes at right angles to the previous year's growth. This operation is repeated every year, and the branches thinned out, so that every line of the stems can be followed. Another favourite and very effective way of training a pine, is to carry a long branch out over a stream or pond, and by skilful training and cutting to give it the direction that, after a few years' growth, will have become natural to it, and the whole strength of the tree will seem concentrated in that one branch. These trees should be placed by the water's edge or on the slope of a hill, and are often planted leaning at all manner of angles. The gardener is never sparing in his use of stout bamboo props, which to our Western ideas would appear unsightly.

It is not in these trees, interesting as they always are, that the admiration of the visitor to a Japanese nursery garden will be centred; for how few foreigners remain long enough in the country, or take sufficient interest in their temporary home, to construct a new garden round it; yet how easy it seems to accomplish, when old gnarled trees are ready grown. It would appear as though a few hours' planning and plotting, a few stones and trees, a few days' work for a few coolies, are all that is required, and the thing would be done; but remember success depends upon the plan, one false touch would set the whole conception ajar, so woe betide the foreigner if he were to attempt to interfere with the making of his garden; left to himself a Japanese is never guilty of that one false touch.

Arranged in rows on wooden platforms will be the object of our visit to the nursery garden—the dwarf trees—whose fame has spread throughout the world, and who seem to share with the cherry blossom the floral fame of Japan. When first I visited the country I went prepared to be disappointed with the dwarf trees; I had seen inferior specimens shipped to Europe no doubt because of their inferiority, pining away a lingering life in a climate unsuited to them, deprived of all care and attention; for an idea prevailed in England when they were first imported, that these tiny trees, the result of years of patient training, required no water, and either no fresh air or else were equally indifferent to the fiery rays of the summer suns or the icy blasts of the winter winds. A visit to a garden in their native country will soon reveal that such is not the case. The trees are not coddled, it is true, but the proper allowance of water, especially

NURSERY GARDENS

in their growing season, is most important, and they are impatient of a draught; though many seem to stand the full rays of the sun, the best specimens had generally some light canvas or bamboo blinds, arranged so that they could be drawn over the stands during the hottest hours of the scorching summer days. I have heard these trees described as tortured trees; to me, good specimens never gave that impression, their charm took possession of me, and a grand old pine or juniper whose gnarled and twisted trunk suggested a giant of the forest, and yet was under three feet in height, standing in a soft-coloured porcelain bowl, gave me infinite pleasure. I could see no fault in them, they are completely satisfying and give a strange feeling of repose.

Their variety is infinite, from six inches in height to as many feet; pines, junipers, thujas, maples, larch, willows, and, among the flowering trees, pink and white plum, single and double cherries, tiny peach-trees, smothered by their blossoms, pyrus trained in fantastic shapes, all will be there in bewildering choice of beauty. I have heard of a single treasure, a weeping willow, only six inches in height, the reward of years of patience, for which the price of 7000 yen

(£700) was paid; probably to our eyes it would have had no more value than a humble "dwarf" which, in consequence of some slight imperfection, would not fetch more than *sevenpence*. In a perfect specimen not only each branch, but each twig and each leaf, must conform absolutely in direction and proportion to the same unbending laws which govern this art, as well as its sister arts of landscape gardening and flower arrangement—laws which a writer says were "the iron rules laid down by the canons of taste in the days when Iyeyasu Tokugawa paralysed into an adamantine immobility the whole artistic and intellectual life of the country." So in every garden there will be failures as perfect works of art, but beautiful in our eyes, which fail to see any difference between the perfect specimen with its boughs bent down by the weight of the laws which have trained it and priced it at some hundred yen, or the "failure" by its side, beautiful and wonderful, with all its imperfections an exquisite and dainty thing, priced at as many pence.

Perhaps one of the best opportunities for buying these imperfect trees, which are still admired and readily bought by the Japanese themselves, though not to be treasured as works of art, is at

THE OLD WISTARIA

NURSERY GARDENS

the sales which take place at night in the streets of Kyoto on certain days of the month. The plants are arranged on stalls down each side of a narrow street, and the intending purchaser has to fight his way through a dense crowd to choose his plants. No lover of dwarf trees should miss attending one of these sales, and perhaps the uncertainty as to whether the plant is in good health, or the bowl containing it is broken, adds to the excitement of bargaining with the stallholder; every Japanese loves a bargain, and the transaction is eagerly watched by the crowd, and the "foreign devil" will gain their admiration if he can hold his own against the rapacity of the salesman. As the plants vary in price, from a few sen to two or three yen, one can afford to carry off a sufficient number to ensure having some, at least, that will be a reward for one's patience. On the 1st of April the best night-market of the year is held. The stalls will be covered with tempting little flowering trees, their buds almost bursting and full of promise of lovely blossoms to come—sturdy little peach-trees, their branches thickly covered with soft velvet buds just tinged with pink; drooping cherries wreathed with red-brown buds; slender pyrus trained into wonderful twisted shapes; little groves of maple-trees, their scarlet or bronze leaves just unfurling, or miniature forests of larch, shading mossy ravines with rivers of white sand; ancient pine-trees spreading their branches over rocky precipices rising from a bed of pebbles; sweet-scented daphnes, golden-flowered forsythias, and early azaleas in porcelain dishes, which are round or oval, square, shallow or deep, and of every shade, from white, through soft greys and blues to a deep green. Every plant is a picture in itself, and the difficulty lies in deciding, not which to buy, but which one can bring oneself to leave behind.

Siebold, who visited Japan and wrote the *Flora Japonica* upwards of sixty years ago, thus describes the dwarf trees :—

The Japanese have an incredible fondness for dwarf trees, and with reference to this the cultivation of the Ume, or Plum, is one of the most general and lucrative employments of the country. Such plants are increased by in-arching, and by this means specimens are obtained which have the peculiar habit of the Weeping Willow. A nurseryman offered me for sale in 1826 a plant in flower which was scarcely three inches high; this *chef d'œuvre* of gardening was grown in a little lacquered box of three tiers, similar to those filled with drugs which the Japanese carry in their belts; in the upper tier was this Ume, in the second row a little Spruce Fir, and at the lowest a Bamboo scarcely an inch and a half high.

The Japanese still love their dwarf trees as much as they did in the days of Siebold, and the trade in them has received additional impetus of late years, as great numbers are exported annually to Europe and the United States, where I fear they are not treasured as works of art, but are only regarded as curiosities.

At different seasons of the year the nursery gardens will be gay with the display of some especial flower. Early in May the gaudy-coloured curtains and paper lanterns at the gates will announce, in the bold black lettering which is one of the chief ornaments of the country, that a special exhibition of azaleas is being held. It is scarcely conceivable that any plants can bear so many blossoms as do these stiff and prim little azalea-trees; the individual blooms are small, but their serried ranks form one dense even mass, flat as a table, for no straggling branches are allowed in these perfectly grown plants. Every shade is there, an incredible blaze of colour, all the plants the same shape, all practically the same size, and all in the same shaped pots; the only variety being in the delicate hue of the faience pots or the vivid colouring of the blossoms. The pots are arranged in rows or stages under the blue and white checked roofing, which seems peculiarly to belong to flower exhibitions; the effect cannot be said to be artistic, but there is something very attractive about the little trees, which are visited by the same crowd of sight-seers, who seem to spend their days in "flower-viewing" and quiet feasting on the matted benches, the latter being inseparable from these flower resorts.

Other flower exhibitions will follow in their turn—great flaunting pæonies, brought with loving care from the gardens near Osaka; and then the last and most treasured flower of all, the chrysanthemum. Again the little matted or chess-board roof will be brought into requisition, and an unceasing throng of visitors will discuss the merits of the last new variety, or of a plant more perfectly grown than its neighbour. Here, too, I saw plants of single chrysanthemums, like great soft pink daisies, grown in tall narrow porcelain pots, grey-blue in colour; left untrained and unsupported the main stem fell over the side of the pot, and the whole plant hung down with natural grace; the effect was charming, and I could not help thinking might easily be accomplished in any garden.

At the end of the year may also be seen the dishes being prepared with a combination of

NURSERY GARDENS

plum, bamboo, and pine which will be found on the *tokonoma* of almost every house throughout the empire at the New Year, bringing good luck and long life to the inmates. Sometimes the combination will be merely a flower arrangement, but usually it is of a more lasting nature, and a little plum-tree covered with soft pink buds, a tiny gnarled old pine, and a small plant of bamboo, will be firmly planted in the dish, a rock and a few stones may be added for effect, and the ground mossed over to suggest great age. Occasionally a clump of some everlasting flower, such as *Adonis amurensis*, is used instead of the plum.

It is probably in the nursery garden that the traveller will first see one of the toy gardens called *Hachi-niwa*—dish gardens—where a perfect landscape and a well-known scene is accurately represented within the limited area of a shallow china dish, varying in size from six inches in length to two feet. Here we have another art, for the making of *Hachi-niwa* is almost as much trammelled by rules and conventions as its fellow-arts of flower arrangement and landscape gardening, and the same unbending law of proportion is the first consideration. Just as the landscape gardener chooses the scene which his garden is to represent, in proportion to the size of the ground which the future garden is intended to cover, so the maker of a *Hachi-niwa* must choose his scene in proportion to the size of his dish ; or, as his choice of dishes may be infinite, varying from a few inches upwards, and being in shape round or oval, long and narrow, with square or rounded ends ; so having decided on his landscape, he may then choose his dish. As I had been much attracted by these little miniature gardens, each in itself a perfect picture, I determined to learn something of the manner of their construction and to try and grasp a few of the principles of the art. I had heard of a gardener in Kyoto who was a great master in the art, a disciple and pupil of one of the Tokyo professors, who might tell me what I wished to learn. On my first visit to his house he looked incredulous at the idea of a foreigner wishing to study the art of *Hachi-niwa*. Thinking I could only wish to purchase a ready-made garden to carry off as a curiosity, he appeared decidedly reserved, and reluctant to impart any information on the subject of their composition. A friend who accompanied me, and was more eloquent in his language than I was, assured him that I was in earnest—not merely a passer-by, but one who had already spent many

NURSERY GARDENS

months in his country; then his interest awoke, and he asked me to return the next day, when he would have all the materials prepared and I could choose my own subject.

Many a happy hour did I spend making these little gardens and learning something of their history. A certain paraphernalia is necessary for the construction of these miniature landscapes, and the requisite materials include a supply of moss of every variety—close cushions of moss to form the mountains, flat spreading moss to clothe the rocks, white lichened moss to carpet the ground beneath the venerable pine-trees, which in themselves are especially grown and dwarfed, till at the age of four or five years they will only have attained the imposing height of as many inches; leaning and bent pines for the scenery of Matsushima or the garden of Kinkakuji, groves of tiny maples for Arashiyama, and pigmy trees of all descriptions. Finally, there are microscopic toys to give life to the scene—perfect little temples and shrines, in exact imitation of the originals, modelled out of the composition that is used for pottery, baked first in their natural colour, then coloured when necessary and baked again; coolies, pedlars, pilgrims in endless variety, less than an inch in height; bridges, lanterns, *torii*, boats, junks, rafts, mills, thatch-roofed cottages—everything, in fact, that is necessary in the making of a landscape, down to breakwaters for the rivers, made like tiny bamboo cages filled with stones, such as exist at every turn of rivers like the Fuji-kawa. The necessary implements consisted of chop-sticks, the use of which is an art in itself, a trowel suggesting a doll's mason's trowel, a tiny flat-iron for smoothing the surface of the sand, besides diminutive scoops for holding only a few grains of sand, a pair of enlarged forceps for placing the moss, little fairy brooms about two inches long to sweep away sand which may have got out of place, and a sieve of like dimensions to sift white powder for a snow scene, and, finally, a fine water sprayer to keep the moss damp and fresh.

When the selection of the dish has been made—the regulation kind being of white or mottled blue china, in size twelve inches by eight, or eighteen inches by twelve, about one inch deep—and the scene decided upon, damp sifted earth will form the mountains and the foundations in which the rocks are embedded; the hills are carefully carved and moulded into perfect shape; crevasses, down which a torrent of white sand will flow, to represent a river, or a mountain road running between a gorge of terrific rocks, are marked out. Then will come the firm planting of the stones, toy temples, houses, or bridges; the position of the trees is carefully weighed and considered; and last of all comes the sand—sand of a deep grey colour for deep water, lighter in colour for the shallows, yellowish sand for the ground or roads, snow-white granite chips for water racing down from the mossy mountains or dashing against the cliffs, coarser shingle for the beach in sea scenes; and the correct use of all these sands is a history in itself, as all the different coloured varieties come from the different rivers of Japan, and to use the wrong sand to represent water or earth would be an unforgivable crime in the eye of the master.

To show that great men have turned their attention to these little toy gardens, no less an artist than the celebrated Hiroshige, whose colour-prints of the fifty-three stages of the journey on the old Tokaido road, along which the Shoguns, in days gone by, travelled with all the pomp and state due to their rank, from Kyoto to Yedo, are well known and prized by all lovers of these prints, evidently considered these scenes so suited for the making of toy gardens, that he designed a special book in which the fifty-three views appear as

Hachi-niwa. The book is now, unfortunately, scarce and difficult to obtain, but I had the delight of seeing the whole set of views in real life, each in its little dish. My teacher told me that the first Exhibition of *Hachi-niwa* ever held in Kyoto would take place at the Kyoto Club, where the various competitors would exhibit different views, and a prize would be awarded, from votes by ballot, to the best in the collection. Needless to say, as soon as the doors, or rather the sliding *shoji*, of the club were thrown open to the public, I hastened to study these perfect little works of art. Round three white-matted rooms they stood, each dish on a low black wood stand a few inches high, raised on a dais only another few inches from the ground, so that to view them properly it was necessary to kneel in adoration before them. I was asked to vote for the three I liked best, and never did I have a greater difficulty in deciding. At first a view of Kodzu attracted my attention, with its pine-clad cliffs, deep-indented coast line, stony beach with a moored junk, and stretching away in the distance an expanse of pale blue sea, in the offing being a fleet of fishing-boats with sails not more than half an inch in size bellying in the breeze. This seemed to me perfection; every ripple on the water was marked in the sand, the crests of the waves white, the shadows a deep blue, and the reflection of the junk in perfect outline—a marvel of neatness and ingenuity. But to the Japanese this did not appeal; they condemned it for its very perfection; any one, they said, could make such a scene who had sufficient patience and neat fingers; whereas the view of Kanaya appealed to them as having something grand and yet simple in its conception. A river of white sand threaded its way through the mossy plain, and in the distance stood the little mountain village nestling at the foot of a range of mountains carved in stone. This was awarded the prize, and, I was glad to think, had been made by my teacher. Such an exhibition I had expected would be principally visited by women and children, as I had heard that the making of *Hachi-niwa* was a favourite occupation for the ladies of Tokyo, but here in Kyoto they found interest in the eyes of "grave and reverend seigneurs" who gathered in groups about the rooms. I saw all the members of the club, politicians, writers, poets, the greatest in the land, engrossed in discussing the merits or demerits of toy gardens, and I could not help thinking that here was a country indeed where "small things amuse great minds."

CHAPTER V

TEMPLE GARDENS

Of all the gardens in Japan, and surely in no other country are there so many different forms of gardening, the temple garden, or often the garden surrounding some mouldering Buddhist monastery, remains a peaceful, secluded spot, recalling the Old Japan and days gone by. Unluckily many of them are fast falling into decay, like the buildings they surround; but perhaps it is better so, as they would surely suffer at the hands of the restorer, just as many of the temples have suffered; and though little may remain of the original gardens, the stones, beautified possibly by time, are still the same; the trees may have grown old and gnarled, but the form of the garden remains unchanged.

It has been said that every good garden should be a "modulation from pure nature to pure art," and no one seems to have understood the saying better

AT KITANO TENJIN

TEMPLE GARDENS

than the makers of these old temple gardens: they are always a setting for the building they surround, adding to its grandeur, never dwarfing it; the placing of every stone, the curve of every walk, the shape of the pond, all seem to have been duly weighed and considered, and the result is an harmonious whole.

The grand Nikko temples, the shrines in Uyeno or Shiba, have been left in their natural surroundings; the tall grey masts of the cryptomerias stand like sentries to guard their precious treasure, the avenues broken only by long vistas of enormous steps or the uprights of a colossal granite *torii*. Nothing could be more imposing, and the effect of the bronze green of the cryptomerias against the splendid colour of the temple gives the crowning touch to a picture which in itself alone is worth travelling many thousand miles to see.

At Uyeno the cherry-trees reign all supreme, they do their full work; the mixing of other shrubs or trees would be unnecessary and meaningless; this is the simplest and yet the grandest form of gardening; a few large bronze lanterns and grey stones help to show off the delicate pink of the blossoms when they are in their glory, and yet seem to be part of the temple itself, as no temple or shrine is complete without some of these beautiful votive offerings.

At Nara, again, the cryptomeria forms the principal setting; in spring, many of the trees are wreathed with wistaria, the royal *fuji*, but this only helps to enhance their colour, and is suggestive of a grey misty vapour rather than a real flower, as often one sees no trace of the stem of the wistaria, and one wonders how the mass of mauve flowers has managed to appear suddenly at the very top of one of those giants of the forest.

It is not around these large and world-renowned temples that one finds a garden, in the sense that we Europeans regard a garden, but rather in some peaceful spot which seems to have been overlooked by the hustle and bustle of the large town in which it may be situated. I am thinking now of one such garden in Kyoto; the evening bell seems to call you to come within its sanctuary, and once there one would surely never leave until the final closing of its great outer wooden door sends the loiterer away. It has an irresistible charm this tiny garden, hardly more than a toy compared to the scale of our English gardens, and it was no surprise to me to learn that it was planned to suggest in miniature the

THE DROOPING CHERRY

TEMPLE GARDENS

fabulous Garden of Paradise. One enters its outer precincts through one of those solid wooden gateways which seem so fitting to guard their charge, wood guarding wood, for remember all temples are made of wood in Japan; though many different kinds may be used, and the rarer and more beautifully veined pieces are brought together and collected from far and wide, still it is all wood, and for that reason the buildings seem to be especially in keeping with a garden.

On either side of the gateway stand two old pine-trees, carefully trained and thinned at the proper season; but the most beautiful guardian is just within the gate, a grand old weeping cherry-tree, in April its boughs bent down by the weight of its blossoms, while its glory lasts for a week or two, casting a pinky light on all around. Even now you are only being prepared for the beauty to come, as you must knock on yet another little wooden door and ask permission of the acolyte to enter; he will offer to tell you the history of the garden in his peculiar sing-song note, suggesting a recitative, and utterly incomprehensible, unless you have thoroughly mastered his language. Seeing a foreigner he will probably reconcile himself to letting you wander at your will, and enjoy the beauties of this little haven of rest. We are told that the buildings were formerly magnificent, but have suffered from fire at the hands of the *ronins*, and in later days from accidental fires. What remains of the original building seems complete in itself, and one feels one would not have it otherwise. The garden was designed by the celebrated Kobori Enshu, and, like all his work, is much regarded and valued by the Japanese. The plan, roughly speaking, appears to be two ponds, a wooden bridge, and three tiny islands; but to the understanding one, they are the Crane and Tortoise ponds, the two small islands on the south being regarded as a crane, while the northern one is a tortoise. The wooden bridge is a Bridge of Heaven, and contains the *Kwangetsudai*, or Moon-gazing Platform, brought from the Momoyama Palace at Fushimi, where Hideyoshi is said to have used it for that purpose. All this is of deep interest to the Japanese; but to our eyes the charm of the garden lies in the fact that it is a little old-world garden full of repose, suggesting the Old Japan, and spots where foreign feet have seldom trod. I have known this garden at all seasons of the year. In February, when biting snow-showers remind one that winter is not yet over, the moss- and lichen-clad stones, the trim, clean-cut azalea and sweet box bushes, and the carpet of velvety moss in broad patches where the turf has not yet recovered from the winter frosts, are its only adornments. The pink buds of the one plum-tree it contains are fast swelling, and show you that spring's fairy raiment is being prepared by Nature; the buds of the large bush of flame-coloured *Azalea mollis*—possibly the pride of the garden—also help to give promise of future glories.

Kodaiji was once famous for its cherry-trees, but now few remain, and we must content ourselves with its other treasures, which seem to bloom in one never-ending succession throughout the year. July is the only month in which I have never seen this garden, but I feel certain that even then there is no blank, something would spring up to be the pride of the garden. In March her one plum-tree reigns supreme, in April the cherry blossom; in May the Crane pond is fringed with purple irises, and the gorgeous azalea casts its reflection also; in June the later *Azalea indica* . . . . flower as best they can, but how many of their buds fall victims to the gardener's shears. In July the lotus leaves in both the ponds are already getting taller every hour, and in the early hours of some morning late in July the first lotus bud will open with a crack and gradually unfurl its beautiful pink or white blossom. All through August fresh buds will appear, and indeed well into September, when at last the leaves will begin to curl and shrivel, and one can only wonder how they stood the scorching heat of the sun all through those long weeks.

By the beginning of October the leaves of the maples will be turning, gradually growing more and more fiery in colour as the month dies out, till in November they are in all their gaudy splendour, and Kodaiji is noted for its *momiji*. The priest, too, who evidently loves his garden, has by now moved with tender care his chrysanthemum plants, whose pots have been kept from the sun's fiercest rays, and never allowed to cry out for water, and placed them in one of those curiously fragile little structures which seem to exist only for the protection of chrysanthemums, with a roof more suggestive of a chess-board than anything else, and arranged them in front of his dwelling-room, so that he can sit and gaze at them, just as in old days Hideyoshi sat on the neighbouring platform to gaze at the moon. Do not imagine

A SHRINE AT KYOMIDZU

that when the last maple falls, or the last *kiku* flower is cut, the year is over in this favoured little spot, for in December the *Camellia Sasanqua* holds its own against frost and even snow; its lovely rose-coloured flowers, which with their yellow stamens, are more suggestive of the blooms of Penzance briar roses than of camellias, are in sharp contrast with the deep glossy foliage, and seem more fitted for a spring flower than one for the dying year.

It is not always easy for the foreigner to obtain permission to visit some of these secluded and hallowed spots. I can recall a long rough ricksha drive in the environs of Kyoto, through somewhat uninteresting country, consisting of endless miles of rice-fields—Hiezan, it is true, forming a beautiful background; but though I was armed with credentials which I was assured would gain me admission to a veritable holy of holies, a garden so old that no one knew its origin, my enthusiasm was beginning to wane when we arrived within some large rambling temple grounds. We asked to see the garden, and were bowed into a not very interesting and rather uncared-for court, but I felt this could not be the spot I had come so far to see; besides, admission had been too readily granted; it would require patience and perseverance to find this inner sanctuary. After many explanations and many times being assured there was no other garden, we were eventually directed to the priest's private dwelling, and then I knew my chance had come, as an especially holy man was the owner of the precious little garden. I was greeted with a look of horror and incredulity: "Was it possible that the foreigner had even penetrated within these mouldering monastery grounds?" The permission was granted, and I entered the spotlessly clean white-matted rooms, which all looked on the garden. First a little forecourt, and beyond, the sacred spot. At the first glance what did it consist of? A few stone lanterns, almost diminutive in size, to be in keeping with the rest of the garden; some so buried in velvety moss that their shape seemed almost altered by the thickness of their green canopy; a few curiously shaped and fantastic stones, also with their covering of grey lichen and moss; some old gnarled and twisted shrubs, and two or three little toy stone bridges. Not a single flower to break the severity of the outline. The garden lay in a pine wood, and at first I thought, "How curious that a spot so evidently well cared for should be carpeted thickly

WHITE CHERRY AT KITANO

with pine needles!" Never had I seen stone bridges placed where there was no water to cross; the only water in the garden appearing to be a tiny little ceaseless trickle in the beautifully shaped water-basin, which stands at the entrance to nearly all Japanese gardens, however small; but presently I noticed that the pine needles only covered the actual ground, not one was lying on the little rising mound or lodging in any bush, and then I realised the cleverness, the ingenuity of the idea— the pine needles represented the water; each spine seemed to be in its place under the little bridge; they came perfectly smooth and always following each the same way like flowing water. Presently some projecting point or little island in this fancy lake would break their regularity, and they would be turned and twisted to represent the current of the water. It took one's breath away. "Who ever had the patience to arrange this carpet?" It seemed almost as if it might be the work of some one undergoing a penance, being condemned to keep these pine needles in perfect order; one puff of wind might mean hours of work to their guardian. I felt that my perseverance had been well repaid, as during all my wanderings in Japan I never came across another example of that style of gardening, nor was I ever able to obtain the real history of this garden.

The gardens round the smaller temples seem generally to be in the special care of some old priest. Many of them unfortunately are fast falling into decay, and are often neglected; but many are evidently the pride and joy of their owner, who usually seems much gratified by the admiration they evoke. Often only a very small piece is kept in anything like trim and formal order, and then one wanders up the hill and finds a different scene—nature running riot, helped by a minute mountain stream, as an unceasing supply of moisture seems almost more necessary to the vegetation of Japan than to that of any other country; but still the path winds on, and the wanderer is impelled to see where it will lead him to. The end is always the same, some silent graveyard—perhaps only a score or so of memorials of the dead, or perhaps hundreds, or even it would seem almost thousands, of these ghostly moss-blackened monuments, jostling each other, so crowded are they, hardly any two alike in size or shape, leaning all of them, suggesting endless earthquakes, but mostly with a section of bamboo in front of them to hold a branch of evergreen or flower, showing

TEMPLE GARDENS

that some one still remembers the departed one, and loving hands light the humble incense bowl.

Perhaps one of the most elaborate gardens I ever saw was that of Sampo-in, on the way to Otsu. Here one feels as if the work of man had almost distorted nature, if such a thing were possible, and yet the picture would be poor indeed were it not for its splendid setting of forest trees. Again a giant weeping cherry stands like a guardian within the gate, and then you pass on; and never have I seen trees so fantastically twisted into the most impossible angles and shapes. The keynote of the garden seems to be the lilliputian mountain torrent, for does not that give a *raison d'être* for the stone or turf bridges which are flung across it to connect the mossy banks with the diminutive islands, on one of which stands a celebrated pine, twisted, and torn, and cut, so that it has lost all trace of what nature intended it to be, but surely not lost all charm. In this garden also there are no flowers, only little trespassers. I noticed numbers of little wild flowers nestling in the shadow of the bridges or between the mossy rocks, seeming to pray to be left undisturbed by the ruthless weeder. The pride of this especial garden was its maples. When I saw it, they had not yet lost the red glow in which their leaves unfurl in spring; but in November they would doubtless be better still, and the garden illuminated by a blaze of colour. On leaving, it seemed impossible to avoid marring the patterns traced in the silver sand, patterns of a thousand years ago.

Round some of the larger and more imposing temples and monasteries the ground is less a garden than a pleasaunce, for the little miniature gardens I have described would be no fitting framework, for instance, for that noble building the Chion-in in Kyoto, whose grounds include some sixty acres on the wooded slope of those hills which form an unrivalled background to the fairest city of Japan. So large an extent could not possibly be broken up and formed into a garden such as I have already described; the effect would be grotesque and all sense of true proportion lost. How imposing is the great gate standing in its setting of pines, in spring softened by the cherry blossom which shows here and there between them. A long dizzy flight of stone steps leads up to the main building of the temple. Here the ground has been levelled, the work of many thousand hands, it being no petty task to level a plateau large enough for the main building of this mighty edifice, some

CHERRY BLOSSOM, CHION-IN TEMPLE

146 feet long and 114 feet wide. Hardly less imposing is the assembly hall or room of a thousand mats, surrounded by a wooden corridor so constructed that in walking round it there is produced a sound which is thought to resemble the singing of the *uguisu*, the Japanese nightingale, and there is yet another grand hall, the Dai Hojo. How grandly and simply the grounds of this temple are adorned. The large square in front of the main building has for its chief adornment two stone lanterns of colossal size, and the celebrated bronze water-basin in the form of a lotus leaf, from whose lip runs a ceaseless stream of clear water brought from the hill above. A few specially beautiful cherry-trees and some grand old pines, leaning most of them, but all the more beautiful for that reason, surround this square, and form a fitting setting to that massive pile. Yet another flight of steps leads to the bell-tower—also a fitting guardian, as more than once the thundering of this mighty bell has summoned all who revered their beloved Chion-in to come and protect it from an imminent danger of fire.

The Japanese are great respecters of legends, which may make a tree or stone sacred for all time. The Melon Rock, *Kwasho Seki*, has been so called from the story that a melon plant sprouted out from beneath the rock and grew so rapidly that in a single night it had covered the whole rock, blossomed, and borne fruit. Many hundred sight-seers trail during their weary tramp to gaze with awe at this plain grey stone inscribed with the characters of *Gozu Tenno* or Bull-head Emperor, and we in our turn cannot fail to gaze with respect at their simple faith.

CHAPTER VI

SUMMER FLOWERS

MAY is essentially the flower month in Japan, and a ramble through the country cannot fail to be a never-ending joy and surprise to the flower lover. It was nearly the middle of the flower month when, wearied of the works of man, the glories and splendour of the endless round of temples, museums, theatres, *no* dances, and the usual sights which all new-comers to the country must be introduced to, I started for Matsushima, the land of the pine-clad islands. I had not expected to find flowers there, but rather change of scene and peace. I felt that for a time I must be "far from the madding crowd."

It is a fairy scene which greets the eye in the early dawn after a long and dusty journey, and I had to look and look again to make sure that these tiny phantom islands were real and solid, not merely shadows on the water, or even a moored junk, which presently would pass on and vanish from the scene. As the sun rose higher the islands stood out clear in the yellow morning light, then one realised why they are called collectively Matsushima—Pine Islands,—for, however tiny it may be, each isle has to support its burden of twisted, bent, and leaning trees. How the seed has ever found the crannies and cracks between the rocks in which to ripen, and eventually develop into those fantastic trees, was a never-ending source of marvel and admiration to me. Think of the cruel winter snows, and storms blowing in from the Pacific, that these trees have had to withstand from their earliest infancy; small wonder that some appear to have more spreading roots than branches. Many an idle day was spent exploring this little host of islands, some with their rosy carpet of azalea, perhaps not more than a few inches high, creeping along close to the ground as if seeking protection from the fierce winter gales. None the less beautiful for being dwarfed, it seemed rather as though this fiery pink azalea had taken the place of ground ivy, and what a beautiful *remplaçant*! On other islands the wild wistaria had flung its long vine-like branches from tree to tree, and suggested the lianes of a tropical forest; one scrambled knee-deep in many of the hardier ferns to attain the summit of Ogidani, in order to gaze across the whole lagoon and out to Kinkwosan; shrubs of bird-cherry were in all their glory; and many others unknown to me helped, in this month of flowers, to make them not only pine-clad but flower-clad islands. It was with genuine regret that I left behind this enchanted land, and with the cries of "*Sayonara*" and "Please come again" ringing in my ears I turned my back on the Toyo Hotel and its hospitable owner; but time was slipping by, and though it would have been easy to dream away months here, I feared I might become a mere loafer, so, after watching the sun set one evening late in May, I returned once more to the railway, and the commonplace.

The train took me back to Itsunomiya through wilder country than I had ever seen on any other railway line in Japan. Bandai San stood glowering and threatening in the distance, and we sped past pine-clad ridges and mountain streams, down to the lower land where glowing rose-coloured azalea seemed to grow as hazel or hornbeam undergrowth in England. One flashed past broad stretches of colour, growing fewer and smaller where the ruthless hand of the cultivator had no doubt found out that the fertile soil would grow other things more profitable, but how far less beautiful, than wild crimson *satsuki*. I was bound for Nikko on an "azalea pilgrimage," for surely every traveller should not fail to see the Nikko azaleas in all their glory, and later in the year the maples, which vie with the cryptomerias for the palm of beauty. The glorious avenue of cryptomerias which lined the old road to Nikko has suffered from the hands of time and man; but long stretches of the splendid old trees still remain, and form a fitting approach to the little mountain village, celebrated throughout the length and breadth of the world for its mortuary shrines, whose final peacefulness and simplicity seem so striking after the ornate splendour and gorgeous colouring of the outer gates and temples.

But it was azaleas, not temples, that I had come to see this time at Nikko, and surely no one could be disappointed. Climbing up the hill, every shade from delicate pink to clear red, pale transparent yellow, and even rosy purple, seems to have run riot in a veritable feast of colour. Little shrines nestle by the path, perhaps sheltering a small stone image of Jizo the Helper, the travellers' and the children's God; so we ask his kindly aid, and add our contribution to that of hundreds of other travellers, and pause to gaze by his side at the landscape—across the valley where the river threads its way, now a harmless-looking stream, but in autumn to be swollen into a dangerous roaring torrent, sweeping along, leaving death and destruction in its wake. The azaleas here are not the *satsuki* of Matsushima, but the Azalea Beni Renge, leafless as yet, as the flowers seem so thick upon their stems they leave no room for leaves. Their honeysuckle scent filled the air, and hither and thither darted huge black butterflies, looking strangely like humming-birds, only pausing for a second to suck a drop of honey, and then on again to another, perhaps more freshly opened flower. I noticed these same black butterflies always haunt red or deep pink flowers. Is it vanity on their part—are they stopping to think how admirably the colour contrasts with their own glossy black wings? Then I remembered that the first time I ever saw a humming-bird it was darting from one crimson hibiscus flower to another. Was that also vanity? Or have crimson flowers sweeter or more delicately flavoured honey than the rest?

As the mountain road winds higher and higher

above Nikko, on its way to Chuzenji, we left behind this variety of azalea, and came upon another quite unknown to me. At first I thought the mountain-sides were covered with peach-trees, whose blossoms lingered on in the higher or bleaker regions, but it was not so, all was azalea; some so tall that their bare stems stretched high among the other trees, before they got enough light and air to wreathe their branches with the peach-coloured blossoms. On these, lichen seemed to take the place of leaves; the effect is indescribable to one who has not seen it: the soft greenish-grey tufts clothe the stems, which might without their furry covering look lean and bare; but all this beauty suggests weeks of autumn rain and damp heat, more healthy for plant life than for man. Often the path would be strewn with freshly fallen blossoms, and there overhead one could see the pink flowers against the sky. The banks and moorland were full of tender shoots and buds of shrubs and flowers, which in July will be an endless source of surprise and delight to the wild-flower hunter.

Leaving Nikko behind in all its gay clothing, I bent my steps towards the Watanase valley, one of Japan's most beautiful valleys. The early summer

THE KOBAI PLUM BLOSSOM

is indeed a harmony in greens; the maples had hardly lost their spring colouring when I started in the early dawn from Ashio to follow the course of the river which dashes down some hundred feet or more below the road with a thundering roar, and certainly the valley well deserves its celebrity. The Paulonia trees were then in all their beauty, and side by side with great masses of their purple flowers the wild *fuji* wreathed the trees with its delicate mauve blossoms, until at last I felt that the valley ought to be called the "purple valley." A few tree pæonies were shedding their last petals in a tiny garden where we stopped to rest and sip the inevitable little cup of pale green tea, reminding one that summer had come and spring was gone, not to come again until the scorching summer months, the autumn storms, and winter snows had come and gone.

In early summer the higher moorlands afford a happy hunting-ground for the flower collector. Purple iris and white rue seem to fight their way among the moorland grasses, here and there a Turk's-cap lily raises its scarlet head proudly, the purple bells of the Platycodon are just opening, and the wild white and pink campanula is already fading. The columbine, not the glorified hybrid

Aquilegia of our English gardens, but the humble pale-coloured wild columbine with its long spurs and delicate fern-like foliage; yellow valerian, mauve and white funkias, pink spiræas, Solomon's seal, endless varieties of orchises, and in favoured districts the pale pink *Cypredium macranthum* are among the summer wild flowers, scattered over the plain or nestling on the banks of the mountain streams. The flowering shrubs seemed endless; think how many shrubs introduced into Europe of late years are "japonica"! all these find their homes in one district or another. Besides all the varieties of plum, cherry, and peach, in spring the andromeda bushes are laden with their white bell-flowers, suggestive of a waxy lily of the valley, to be followed by their young leaves as bright as any flowers; every variety of crabs, white deutzias, spiræas, weigelias, the wild white syringa, which also seemed to differ from our garden variety, save only in its delicious odour; and a form of *Rhincospernum jasminoides* which I had not seen before, whose heavy scent filled the air at sundown. All these I can recall having come across during my summer rambles, and doubtless there are many more.

In the later summer months I wandered along

SUMMER FLOWERS

the beautiful coast of the province of Izu, which again seemed to be a home of flowers. The tall spikes of *Bocconia cordata* reared their heads proudly wherever they had escaped the hand of the destroyer; apparently the plant is regarded by the country people as either poisonous or unlucky, as often a splendid clump of it, its height showing how thoroughly it appreciates the deep rich soil, will be here to-day and gone to-morrow, cut off and trampled down with evident intention. This coast seemed to be the home of the hydrangea and also of many different varieties of lilies. In May, on the lower ground of Hiezan, and especially in the neighbourhood of Lake Biwa, the pale pink *Lilium Krameri* may be found in tufts nestling under the shadow of some sheltering shrub, and scattered throughout the district the various forms of *Lilium umbellatum*, but the province of Izu seems to have soil more suited to the late summer lilies. By the middle of July the big buds of the *Lilium auratum* will be fighting their way among the rank growth along the roadside, and in a few days the air will be filled with their scent. Often I was attracted by their fragrance, perhaps all the more remarkable in a land which, alas! is not famed for sweet smells, and then far above one's head, hanging defiantly out of reach, could be seen a single splendid bloom of this king among lilies. They seem to love the shelter and dampness of the wood, where the falling leaves each autumn make a fresh covering for their bulbs. Once I tried to see how deep in the earth the bulbs were buried, but I did not succeed in getting down low enough, and could only tell, from the mark on the stem of the lily which had been pulled, that about eight to ten inches seemed to be the usual depth of the bulb. Often the stems seemed to bear only one splendid bloom, but I was told that was only because the bulbs were young, and even in their wild state from six to eight perfect blooms on one head were not uncommon. There appeared to be every variety of *auratum*, and I noticed that the broad-leaved *platyphyllum* seemed even more sturdy than the rest, the foliage a deeper green, and the individual blossoms more perfect, the markings more distinct, and their scent, if such a thing were possible, even stronger and more overpowering than the more slender-growing *Auratum virginale*.

Then there were the *Rubro Vittatum* with their band of pink down each petal, but never in a purely wild state did I see it so deep in colour and truly defined as in the cultivated form which

LILIUM AURATUM

is exported under that name. It was in the cottage gardens that I saw the finest lilies, and many a giant bearing from twenty to thirty unblemished blooms, at the top of a stem some six or seven feet high, clad with equally unblemished foliage, was brought to me, as it soon became known that the "foreigner" staying at Atami had come especially to see their *yuri no hana*. Not that the Japanese seem ever especially to admire them, and they are not included among their "seven beautiful flowers of late summer." Mr. Parsons gives an example of this fact:—

I was walking one day at Yoshida with a Japanese artist, a remarkable man, who was engaged in making a series of steel engravings, half landscape, half map, of the country round Fuji, and called his attention to a splendid clump of belladonna lilies growing near an old grey tomb; but he would not have them at all, said they were foolish flowers, and the only reason he gave me for not liking them was because they came up without any leaves. When we got back to our tea-house he took my pen and paper and showed me what were the seven beautiful flowers of late summer: the convolvulus, the name of which in Japanese is "asago," meaning the same as our "morning glory"; wild chrysanthemum; yellow valerian; the lespedeza, a kind of bush clover; *Platycodon grandiflorum* and purple blue campanula; *Eulalia japonica*, the tall grass which covers so many of the hills; and *shion*, a rather insignificant aster. I noticed that some versions of the seven flowers differed from his; a large flowered mallow is often substituted for the last he named. There are doubtless different schools which hold strong views on the subject, but on the "morning glory" and some others they are evidently agreed.

The tiger lilies were in bloom in the village gardens, but never in any great number — a clump here and there, for they are seldom allowed to bloom, it is for their bulbs they are cultivated; this is their "edible lily," and young bulbs of *Lilium tigrinum* are among their most prized vegetables. I had noticed a square bed of these lilies suggestive of an asparagus bed, in a priest's garden in Kyoto in May, and thought what a wealth of colour they would provide later in the year; but next time I saw the garden, early in June it may have been, the lilies had all been executed—just their heads cut off,—and when I expressed amazement and regret I was told that this was always done to strengthen the bulb. The variety did not seem to be as fine as those grown under the name of *Tigrinum Fortunii* in England, and yet more robust and with larger heads than our common tiger lily; probably the different soil and damper climate would account for this.

The apricot-coloured *Lilium Batemanni* seemed to know how to protect their bulbs from the hand

LILIES ON THE ROCKS, ATAMI

of the collector, for jutting out between the rocks, hanging perhaps a hundred feet above the sea, these lilies grow, tantalising to those who want to pick them, for these rocks are not easy to climb; but how beautiful they are, their clear colour standing out against the grey cliffs and the restless deep blue sea below.

The cultivation of lilies for exporting seems to have developed into quite an important industry in Japan of late years; the district round Kamakura and right away to Yumoto appeared to be the best soil for their culture. I never saw any *Lilium longiflorum* in their wild state, but thousands, I should think millions, of bulbs of this lily are exported annually, in all its different forms. For indoor growing the variety known as *Harrisii* seems still to be the favourite; though *giganteum* is a stronger form, and certainly is to be preferred for the open ground. *Multiflorum* is for the impatient grower, as it flowers some three weeks earlier, though it is a more slender kind; and there are many others. Even in Japan the dreaded disease among *Lilium auratum* seemed to be not unknown; apparently cultivation brings it in its train, as in fields and gardens I noticed occasionally the fatal yellow leaves, which means death to the bulb; and the other form of disease known as "clubbing" may occur, even when the lilies are growing in their natural state—the two stems grown into one, and the monster head so closely packed with blossoms that none can develop to their full size or beauty; on one head alone I counted over a hundred blooms, but the effect was only that of a poor deformity.

Very beautiful were the large bushes of hydrangea, their branches weighed down by their burdens of immense heads of bright blue flowers. In some parts of England where there is iron in the soil, hydrangeas in the open ground are blue, but what a poor washed-out blue compared to the intensely deep colour of this Japanese variety, *Ajisia Aiyaku*, meaning the blue hydrangea. Their great balls of blossom change from a pale yellow green to bright blue, brighter almost than the sky above, and as they fade, they turn to rosy purple, and back again to a dull green, clinging with ungraceful tenacity to life, as though loth or afraid to die, preferring to rot on their stem rather than drop untimely—unlike the blossoms of spring, ever ready to depart life at the call of nature. A more graceful form is *Hortensis Shirogaku*, with its more loosely formed heads,

AN HYDRANGEA BUSH

never forming a densely packed mass, each individual blossom showing, with the outer petals of a much paler colour in contrast with the deep blue centres. They are moisture-loving plants, as they seem to flourish best on the very brink of the miniature mountain torrents. The garden at Atami known as the Bai-en, celebrated for its early plum blossoms, was gay with great bushes of these shrubs in July; they clothed the banks of the roaring stream, till, as their heads grew heavier, the lower branches were swept by the water.

In the early days of August the hedges and banks in the low country were beginning to look parched and dusty, waiting for the autumn rains, which never fail, and will bring new life and freshness to all the herbage, but not new flowers—the season of wild flowers is nearly gone; though the autumn will bring us the true "lily of the field," the scarlet *Nerine japonica*—a lily of the field, as it is only growing along the edges of the rice patches on neglected banks or nestling among the grey stone tombs of some forgotten graveyard, that you will ever see these lilies. Never in any garden however ill kept, never in any house, and never used as any form of decoration did I see this lily; for are they not the "death flower," the flower of ill omen, or sometimes the "equinox flower," also suggestive of a season full of death and decay. *Nerine* or *Lycoris japonica*, or the spider lily—its name seems difficult to determine—made the land gay in the fading year, gorgeous splashes of colour against the ripening rice, its fringed heads rising leafless from the soil, sometimes in scattered tufts, and sometimes great banks closely covered with their flaunting heads. I felt Japan must indeed be rich in flower treasures for such a one to be overlooked and uncared for. Perhaps in the South of England it might find a home—a resting-place where it would be treasured, not destroyed; at the foot of a grey stone wall a few tufts of this brilliant lily would be a "thing of beauty," though not "a joy for ever."

By November the flower year is over; the last chrysanthemum pots are being hurried under their temporary shelters, away from the danger of the early frost, which any night may turn the country into a blaze of scarlet and gold. Not only the maples will help the year to die in splendour, for so many other trees have as great a variety of colour, though perhaps not quite so brilliant, and the dark leaves of the tulip-trees will presently turn to a sheet of gold, the larch will be shedding its pale yellow spines, while the Japanese oak, *Shira Kashi*, with its ruddy colour will help to relieve the solemn everlasting green of the pines and cryptomerias which clothe the hills. The ripened rice is being quickly stored, and only the grasses and foliage of herbaceous plants are left to give a note of colour to the fields and higher moorland; the tall *Eulalia japonica*, waving in the wind, clothes the golden hills, but will soon be beaten down by the winter snows. So in a blaze of glory the year ends in this Land of Flowers.

CHAPTER VII

PLUM BLOSSOM

IN Japan the flower year begins earlier than in Europe, and while the snow is still lying deep on the ground in the northern provinces, in warm and sheltered districts the *Ume* or plum blossom will clothe the trees with flowers as white as the snow. But in the country round Kyoto or Tokyo it is not until the end of February or the first days of March that the pale pink buds of the plum blossoms will be opening, and there will come a whisper through the air that in a few days the beloved *ume-no-hana* will be in all its glory. The plum is one of the favourite, perhaps *the* favourite tree of the Japanese, so in early March, when the sunny days will remind us that spring is coming, though the cruel frosts and snow showers at night will warn us that winter is not yet gone, every passer-by seems to be talking of *ume*, discussing

VIEWING THE PLUM BLOSSOMS

probably where the earliest blossoms are to be found, and when the first flower-viewing excursion of the year is to take place.

The Japanese are essentially a flower-loving people; in no other country would you find whole families, old and young, rich and poor, tramping for miles in the hot sun or through the drenching rain to indulge in their favourite pastime of flower-viewing. Showing how universal is this custom of special flower-viewing excursions, there is even a phrase in the Japanese language, *hana miru*, meaning to view flowers.

The earliest plum blossom, known as the *no-ume*, is a somewhat uninteresting little white flower, not unlike the wild sloe in our English hedgerows, and I was beginning to think the celebrated plum blossom of Japan was an overrated flower, when gradually its full beauty dawned upon me. The deep pink buds of the later varieties opened into pale blush coloured blossoms, and the crimson buds of the *kobai*—the most cherished of all—burst into a cloud of brilliant pink flowers; others there were, pale lemon coloured or large pure white, in great variety. The plum-tree is especially valued for its age, and a venerable tree, its stems covered with grey lichen, though its flowers may be poor in quality, will be more prized than a young tree with the most brilliant coloured blossoms.

Tsukigase, in the province of Shima, a little village famous for the beauty of its plum-trees, is one of the first places to be visited by that large proportion of the inhabitants of Kyoto who seem to spend most or all their days during the spring months in a never-ending round of sight-seeing and flower-viewing. In the month of March the village is made gay for the reception of these holiday-makers, and undaunted by the bitter winds and vicious scuds of snow which mingle with the falling petals of the *ume*, they will spend long hours in quiet admiration of the mass of blossom which appears to fill the whole valley with a pink and white haze; for over two miles the trees clothe the banks of the river Kizu. Countless tea-stalls are prepared for the guests, light bamboo structures adorned with a few printed linen curtains in soft harmonious colouring, and innumerable paper lanterns suffice for the preparation of a flower feast. Each night, or at the approach of rain, the little maids will carefully pack away the matted benches and these frail decorations under the thatched roof, to be brought forth on the

THE GATE OF THE PLUM GARDENS

PLUM BLOSSOM

morrow or when the storm has cleared. The Japanese regard the flower of the plum with a peculiar reverence, and their feeling for it always seems to be touched with some mysterious sense of sorrow, which perhaps accounted for the fact that these plum-blossom feasts never seemed to attain to the same merry boisterous revels held at the time of the cherry blossom. The people were more quiet and sober in their demeanour; at first I thought their spirits were frozen by the cold, but even the endless drinking of tea and tiny cups of *saké* did not seem to thaw them, and often whole parties, wrapped in their outer winter kimonos, would sit in silent contemplation of the blossoms, warming their hands over that Japanese apology for a fire—an *hibachi*—consisting merely of a pot of charcoal.

In old days the plum blossom was their ideal of purity, an ideal which some attempted to emulate in their lives. The same feelings prevail in China, if we may judge from the poets. This, to be sure, is not surprising, inasmuch as Japan took her literature, like most other things, from the Chinese. The early poems of both countries are much alike, and among them both are many *ume* poems, as the Japanese call them, extolling the beauty and charm of the plum blossom, which ranks as the poet's own flower. Mr. Kango Uchimura has written an ode to it in prose, which contains the following passage:—

> While Spring was still cold I knew that it was at hand by your flowering. You are not Spring, but the prophet of Spring. The cherry blossom is Spring, the iris and the wistaria; but, as each of these has its own season, the gods sent you to keep green our hope of Spring.
>
> I do not say I love you, rather I fear you; you are too dignified; you blossom alone on the branches with no green leaves to bear you company. I do not call you beautiful; your scent is too keen, your petals too stiff. No one will ever sing or dance beneath your boughs. You are the prophet Jeremiah; you are John the Baptist. Standing before you I feel as though in the presence of a solemn master. Yet by your appearance I know that Winter has passed, and that the delightful Spring is at hand. The herald of Spring, you denounce the tyranny of Winter. Your face is stern, but your heart is soft. It is easy to misunderstand you, for, though the daughter of Spring, you wear the garb of a man the man ordained to break the power of cruel Winter.

Two famous men in olden days were particularly associated with the flowers of the plum. One of these was Kajiwara Genda Kagesuge, a great warrior of the twelfth century, who always went into battle carrying in his quiver fresh branches of the blossom, to which, so says the legend, he was indebted for his splendid courage. The other was

Sugawara No Michizane, the minister of the Emperor Ude. The Kwampaku Tokihira, wishing to be quit of the sage's wisdom, sent him into a sort of honourable exile in the island of Kyushu, where he died in 903. After his death came a great reaction in his favour. He was canonised under the name of Tenjin, or the Heavenly god, and to this day he is venerated by all men of letters as their patron saint; in every school the twenty-fifth day of each month is kept as a holiday, and every year on the twenty-fifth of June a great festival is held in his honour. His life is dramatised in the popular play *Sugawara Tenjin Ki*, and all over the land shrines dedicated to his memory rise from groves of plum-trees.

One of the most famous and beautiful of these is the temple of Kitano Tenjin at Kyoto, which has provided subjects for several of the illustrations in this volume. In the inner court of the temple near the splendid two-storied gateway of the Sun, Moon, and Stars stands a large tree of the bright pink blossom, and it would be difficult to find a more beautiful setting for the tree than the background of grey wooden buildings, of which the decorations have been toned by the hand of time into soft mellow hues. In the outer grounds the trees have a background of giant cryptomerias, with long avenues of stone lanterns—votive offerings of every conceivable shape and size—small shrines, and two great granite *torii*, the plain yet majestic gateways which guard the entrance to all Shinto temples. When the trees are in all their glory the flower-viewing parties wander through the grounds in silent admiration, down to the little ravine outside the temple grounds, where the snow-white blossom fills the little valley and clouds of petals fall into the brook below, to be carried away down the stream like drifts of foam. Here may be seen a poet of the old school rapt in thought, composing an ode to the blossom and the nightingale. It is a pretty fancy much honoured in Japan, the plum blossom, the poet, and the nightingale making, they say, the world of beauty complete. For no Japanese ever thinks of the plum blossom apart from the nightingale—which, it should be observed, is not the bird of Keats's poem, singing of summer in full-throated ease, but a little light-winged creature whose favourite haunt is among the flowering branches of this tree.

In Japanese legends the plum blossom and the nightingale are inseparable companions, and repre-

THE TIME OF THE PLUM BLOSSOMS

sent the two spirits of the awakening spring when the mists of winter first begin to roll away. There is a story, for instance, of the daughter of the poet Kino Tsurayuki, who lived in the days of the Emperor Murakami, in the tenth century. From time immemorial a single plum-tree had always stood before the south pavilion of the Imperial Palace at Nara, and when at some period of this Emperor's reign the tree died, messengers were despatched in hot haste to find one worthy to replace it. One was found in the garden of the poet aforesaid, a fine tree with crimson blossoms belonging to his daughter, who was most reluctant to part with her favourite. However, there was, of course, no help for it, and the tree was sent off to the palace grounds with some verses fastened to it, which run thus in Mr. Brinkley's translation—

> Claimed for our sovereign's use,
> Blossoms I've loved so long,
> Can I in duty fail?
> But for the nightingale,
> Seeking her home of song,
> How shall I find excuse?

The Emperor, struck with the graceful sentiment of the verses, made inquiries as to the writer, and finding that she was the daughter of his favourite poet, ordered the tree to be returned to her.

Throughout Japan there is scarcely a district to be found without orchards and groves or temple grounds where the flower-seeker can go to greet spring and the *ume*, but the people of Tokyo are singularly fortunate in their plum orchards. One of the most famous and beautiful is at Sugita, a charming little village nestling by the bluest of waters, near Yokohama, where a thousand trees have stood for upwards of a century, displaying their blossom every spring to admiring eyes from all the country round. Here there are six special kinds of the tree, and their fancy names mark the different characters of the flowers, the Japanese being very clever at finding characteristic names for flowers and trees. The Gwario Bai, or Recumbent Dragon Tree, is the most famous of these, being indeed the most notable thing in the outskirts of Tokyo. Some fifty years ago there grew a wonderful tree of vast age and strange shape, its branches having ploughed up the ground and thrown out new roots in no fewer than fourteen places, thus naturally covering an extensive area. The name of Gwario Bai was given to the tree by old Prince Rekko, who planted the groves in Tokiwa Park in 1837, a piece of forethought highly appreciated by many visitors to this day.

The Shogun (or Generalissimo) of that day also paid a visit to the spot, and made the tree *Goyobaku* or the Tree of Honourable Service, in return for which gracious act of condescension the fruit was presented to him every year. All these honours, however, could not save it from a natural death when its time came; in its place now flourish a number of much less interesting trees, which nevertheless bear the same name, and apparently the same reputation, as their predecessor the Dragon of the prime.

Not far from the Gwario Bai is the orchard of Kinegawa, which can boast an honoured name too, for here the poets come, and you may see perhaps a hundred slips of paper, containing *uta* or *hokku* (seventeen-syllabled) poems, fluttering from the branches. Perhaps here, too, we may find a family party, the mother with the youngest child tightly strapped on her back, its tiny shaven head hardly showing above the wadded quilt which is wrapped closely round it; a little mite of a very few summers, tottering unsteadily on its clogs, clasping a branch of the natural tree adorned with paper blossoms, from which floats a streamer with some strange device, or any of the countless toys which go towards the making of a holiday; and only a few years older a little solemn-faced maiden, whose black beady eyes will glisten with wonder when she is told that she is called *Ume san* after the snow-white blossom at which she has been gazing with awe and admiration. Ume is a common name among Japanese women; they connect it with the ideas of virtue and sweetness, and they are taught to keep the name unspotted during life and to leave it fair after death, even as the scent of the plum blossom smells sweet in the darkness. The following verses are from Piggot's *Garden of Japan* :—

> Home friends change and change,
>   Years pass quickly by;
> Scent of our ancient plum-tree,
>   Thou dost never die.
>
> Home friends are forgotten;
>   Plum-trees blossom fair,
> Petals falling to the breeze
>   Leave their fragrance there.
>
> Cettria's fancy, too,
>   Finds his cup of flowers,
> Seeks his peaceful hiding-place,
>   In the plum's sweet bowers.[1]
>
> Though the snow-flakes hide
>   And thy blossoms kill,
> He will sing, and I shall find
>   Fragrant incense still.

---

[1] Cettria, the nightingale.

Ginsekai is yet another orchard in the neighbourhood of Tokyo, its name signifying Silver World, and on a moonlit night in spring you would say that never was a place more aptly named, if you saw the forest of white blossoms rising out of the snow-clad landscape. There are some pretty verses on the sight, which run thus in English :—

> How shall I find my *ume* tree?
> The moon and the snow are white as she.
> By the fragrance blown on the evening air
> Shalt thou find her there.

It is true that the white varieties of plum blossom have nearly all a most delicious and delicate scent, but the red varieties are quite devoid of any fragrance. The plum is known as one of the Four Floral Gentlemen, the others being the pine, the bamboo, and the orchid. It has flourished in China from time immemorial, where it is known as the Head of the Hundred Flowers, because it is the first to bloom, and it was probably imported from that country through the medium of Korea into Japan. Even that learned botanist the late Dr. Keisuke Ito could not say where the plum-tree first flowered in Japan, nor can any one say with certainty whether *ume* is a Chinese or a Japanese word. Kakimoto no Hitomaro, who lived about the end of the seventh century, was probably the first to celebrate the plum blossom in his verse; and it may be said to have taken rank as a national flower when the Emperor Kwamaru (782-806) planted it before his palace when he moved his capital from Nara to Kyoto.

In those days the word *flower* meant the flower of the plum, just as the word *mountain* meant Hiei san, but it was dethroned from its pride of place when the Emperor Murakami planted the cherry-tree in its stead, and though the plum still stands first with the men of mind, the cherry-tree has ever since been the popular favourite. That the latter is most beautiful cannot be disputed; but for purity of outline, fragrance, and that touch of sadness, which the Japanese profess to find in it, the bloom of the plum is still unrivalled.

There are upwards of three hundred and fifty specimens of the plum, white, pale and bright pink, or even red in colour, single or double in form. Of these the more important are: *Yatsu buse ume*, which derives its name from bearing eight fruits, the blossoms having from two to eight stamens, the word signifying eight tassels; only two or three of these, however, ripen fully, and they are unfit for eating. The *Bungo ume* grows in the Bungo

PLUM BLOSSOM AND LANTERNS

province of the island of Kyushu; its fruit is large and can be eaten uncooked, though the Japanese prefer it pickled or candied. The fruit of the *Ko ume*, celebrated for the beauty of its bright pink blossom, is no bigger than the tip of one's thumb, but has a delicious flavour. *Toko no ume* is a late fruit, clinging to the branch even when fully ripe, whence its name *Toko*, meaning eternal. The flowers of *Suisen ume* have six petals, round or long in shape. *Hava ume*, or the early plum, blooms at the winter solstice.

In no other country does the culture of plants go hand in hand with art as it does in Japan; not only in the case of their dwarf trees, marvels of horticultural art, but even the trees which are necessary for the scenery of their landscape gardens have to conform to the rules which govern the entire art of the country. I remember being shown with great pride by the owner of a tiny garden his one solitary plum-tree, the pride of his garden in those cold March days. It stood leaning over a miniature rocky precipice, down which tumbled a diminutive cascade; old and venerable it looked, having endured ruthless pruning, and only a few large single blossoms clothed its branches. I expressed surprise and some regret that it did not bear more blossoms, and then it was explained to me that many of the buds had been removed, as otherwise the thick cloud of flowers would have hidden the outline of the branches; this was a flight of æstheticism to which I could not rise, and I felt I should have preferred to see the tree bearing its full burden of blossom. This practice of disbudding is also occasionally carried out with old specimens of dwarf plum-trees when it is considered that a wealth of blossom would hide the growth of the little tree, which by careful training has after years of patience rewarded the owner by conforming to the desired shape laid down by the canons of art. These little trees are in great demand at the close of the year, for hardly a house in the land is without a tiny tree of *ume*, to bring luck at the opening of another year; so during November and December, when their pale-pink buds are fast swelling, they are tended with the greatest care, brought into the sun during the day, plentifully watered at sundown, and sheltered from all cold winds. Thus they flower sometimes as early as New Year's Day, to the intense pride and joy of their owners. The hearts of the plum-trees, say the Japanese, are a thousand years old, and yet young as the hopes of Japan.

CHAPTER VIII

PEACH BLOSSOM

THE peach blossom has never attained the fame in Japanese art, or among their poets, that its classical predecessor the plum, or its successor the cherry of patriotic fame, has been honoured with; but it is none the less beautiful for that reason, and its blossoms excel those of the plum in size, richness, and colouring. Towards the end of March the first flowers of the peach-trees will be opening, although long before this time, branches closely covered with the bright-pink buds will have been among the flowers offered for arrangement on the *tokonoma*, as in the warmth of the house (though surely there seems to be very little warmth in a Japanese house all through the long cold March days) the buds will quickly open and last in beauty for many days. These will be branches of the early bright pink variety, but it is not until the beginning of April that the large flowered pure white, double and semi-double flowers of every shade of pink, and even a deep crimson of a remarkably beautiful tone, will be in their full glory, and it is hard to understand why this splendid blossom should be comparatively neglected and relegated to secondary rank by the artist as a decorative motive and material.

The less severely artistic, who find enjoyment at any spot where blossom and colour are to be seen, will visit Momoyama (Peach Mountain) in crowds during the first week in April, and the narrow streets leading up to the hill will be gay with visitors, and among the orchards the little temporary tea sheds will be set out for their comfort and refreshment. So yet another "Feast of blossom" will be celebrated. The trees may perhaps lack some of the grace of the old gnarled plum-trees, and they do not appear to have such a long life, as never did I hear of any very celebrated old specimen trees, but rather groves or orchards of younger trees, which no doubt, in order to make them bloom freely, receive drastic treatment at the hand of the pruner. Very lovely are these groves of peach-trees, and surely they must have found favour in the ancient days, as on Momoyama stood

PEACH BLOSSOM

Hideyoshi's palace, the grandest ever built in Japan, whose spoils in the shape of gold screens and *fusuma* adorn half the temples in Kyoto.

The peach orchards of *Soka-no-momoyama* at Senju are a favourite resort of the Tokyo holiday-makers, who make annual pilgrimages to do honour to the peach blossoms, and parties sit feasting on the matted benches; here and there perhaps a group discussing the politics of the capital, or a solitary poet composing a *hokku* on the peach blossom, or a family party; and there the little boys and girls, decked out in their brightest-coloured kimonos and obis in honour of the holiday, will be listening with rapt attention to the fairy-story of Momo Taro, who jumped out of a large peach-stone. To the older children it is an old story, for every Japanese child has listened at bedtime to the tale of Momo Taro told by its mother, but for the little ones this may be their first year of "peach-viewing" and understanding, and their eyebrows will rise in amazement when they hear the history. "Once upon a time," the story says, "there was an old man and an old woman; the old man went up the mountain to collect dried brushwood, and the old woman went to the river to wash clothes," and there one of the older boys will interrupt, I am sure, saying, "A big peach came down the river; and Momo Taro jumped out of the stone when the old woman brought it home and cut it open, didn't he?" So there is not a child in Japan who does not know the history of Momo Taro, the children's hero, who made an expedition into the Oniga Shima (Devil's Island) followed by his dog and monkey servitors. It would be no surprise to them to see even a fat little boy like themselves spring out of the end of the fruit, so the Japanese boys adore the peach; and the little girls share their affection for it, as it is always associated in their mind with their own especial festival.

During the season of the early peach blossoms (on 3rd March) the Girls' Festival (*Jōmi-no-sekku*) is celebrated throughout Japan; it is also called the Feast of Dolls (Hina Matsuri), and the Peach Festival, for no Girls' Festival is complete without some branches of peach blossom in the vase on the *tokonoma*. This day is eagerly looked forward to by every little girl in Japan, from the highest to the lowest in the land, for every house possesses its little store of dolls, only to be brought out and exhibited with due pomp and ceremony on this one day in the year. In the houses of the rich, the Dairi Hina — tiny models of people and their belongings — the dolls will be dressed in gorgeous silk, and their accessories mostly made of priceless lacquer. The whole ancient Japanese Court in miniature there may be: these will all be displayed on the *tokonoma* of the guest chamber, possibly on a piece of brocade as gorgeous as the peach blossom in colour. And there you will see an emperor and an empress and a set of Court musicians; before them the most elaborate dinner sets in ancient form; beside them there will be the *Sho kudai* (lamp-stand with paper shade) with pictures of peach blossom on it. The little daughters of the house will surely look to our eyes only like larger dolls, with their delicate coloured silk crepe kimonos and stiff brocade obis standing out like great butterflies on their backs, their hair carefully dressed according to their age, the older ones with just a little powder on their tiny inscrutable faces, acting as hostesses with all the solemn grace of their mother, offering to the guests tiny cups of tea and little fairy cakes shaped and coloured like peach petals. This girls' day is one of the prettiest sights in Japan, and yet there is no record how far back the festival originated, though it is believed to date from a thousand years ago. In the days of the Tokugawa feudal régime

—days of perfect peace and prosperity—it became a very expensive festival, and great sums were expended on these toy Dairi Hina, so it is not surprising that they were handed down as heirlooms in families only to be displayed once a year, or sometimes a bride, scarcely more than a child herself, would take her set of favourite dolls with her to her husband's house, so that her little daughter might perhaps some day also use them to celebrate the Girls' or Peach Festival. So in Japan the peach is truly the children's tree.

Momo, meaning a hundred, is considered "emblematic of longevity and perfection," which probably is the origin of the story of Seibo the fairy who governed the western realm of China. She gave some peaches to the Emperor Butei, and told him that that variety of peach only bore fruit once in three thousand years, and he would live eternally from the fruit's heavenly influence. If we could only get such peaches to-day? Perhaps it might do as well to eat a common peach from the market and dream, if possible, of the beauty of eternal life and be happy.

In Chinese art the peach blossom seems to rank higher than it does in Japan, and a very favourite subject with Chinese artists is an ox in a peach orchard. The finest pot-grown peach-trees I ever saw were in China, their gnarled stems looking truly a thousand years old, their branches trained and bent or merely drooping like a willow, covered with the clear pink blossoms. The trunks of these fine old trees may have been three or four feet high; but in Japan it is possible to procure a little plant for perhaps 25 sen (about sixpence) whose branches are so tightly packed with blossoms it is impossible to see a trace of even the bark between them—a perfect little tree in a delicate green or mottled blue porcelain pot. I could not help thinking what pleasure such trees would give in England, but apparently it is only the Japanese who know the real secret of growing them, the exact shoots to leave and which to cut away, to ensure this wealth of blossom. I felt in England my little peach-tree would only flower here and there, and its beauty would be lost.

There is a popular saying in Japan, *Momo kuri san nen, kaki hachinen*, meaning "three years for peach and chestnut, eight years for persimmon." The peach-tree is of rapid growth; this fact is proved by there being a variety called *Issai momo*, because it blooms the first year of its growth, and bears fruit the second. There is *Futairo momo*, the two-coloured peach, whose blossoms are mingled red and white in colour, single and double in petals; there is *Hiku momo*, or chrysanthemum peach, as its blossoms are the shape of a chrysanthemum flower, in clusters of twelve or thirteen; the camellia peach and many others with fancy names from their supposed resemblance to their god-father. The native peaches do not bear good fruit, and the better varieties have been introduced from America, but up to now with only moderate success. There are no good eating peaches in Japan; this may be the fault of the climate, possibly the hot damp summer does not suit them, or the cultivation may be at fault; but when their blossoms provide such a feast of colour and beauty it seems altogether too unromantic and too material to worry over the texture and flavour of the fruit.

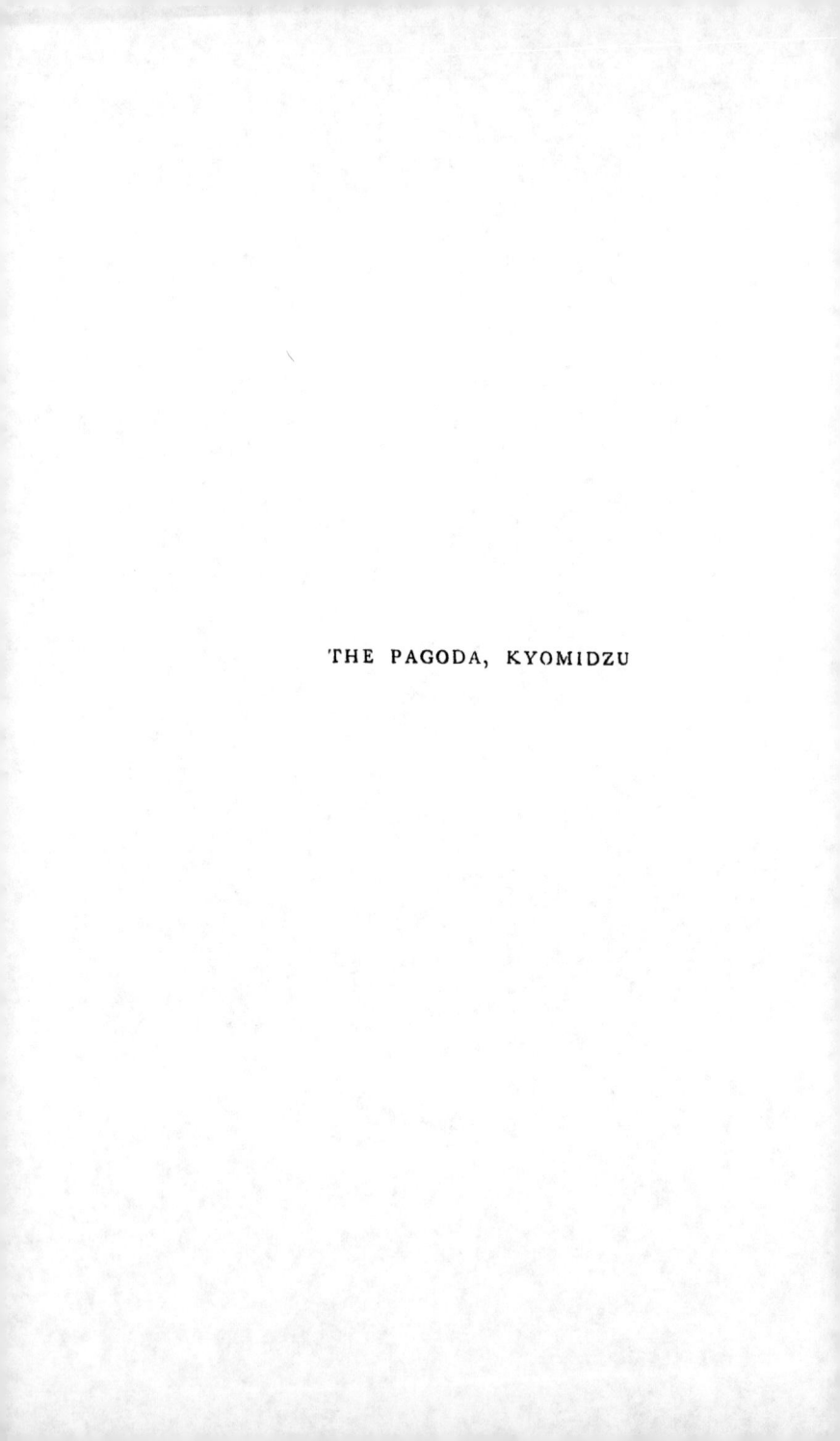

THE PAGODA, KYOMIDZU

CHAPTER IX

CHERRY BLOSSOM

JAPAN is often called "The Land of the Cherry Blossom," and it is true that for centuries their *Sakura-no-hana* has been the favourite flower of the Japanese. The refinement and grace of its beauty appeals to them so intensely, that the month of April, the time of the cherry blossom, might almost be regarded as a national holiday throughout the country; and can one wonder that a whole nation should forget for a time their work and domestic worries in the innocent enjoyment of sitting under the flower-laden trees?

In contrast to the simple growth of the plum-tree, the blossom of the cherry covers the whole tree in rich profusion, the branches bending under the weight of its luxuriance, scattering a rosy shower of petals as they sway in the spring breezes. Lafcadio Hearn, in his *Glimpses of Unfamiliar*

Japan, says: "When, in spring, the trees flower, it is as though fleecy masses of clouds, faintly tinged by sunset, had floated down from the sky, to fold themselves about the branches. . . . The reader who has never seen a cherry-tree blossoming in Japan cannot possibly imagine the delight of the spectacle. There are no green leaves; these come later; there is only a glorious burst of blossoms, veiling every bough and twig in their delicate mist; and the soil beneath each tree is covered deep out of sight by fallen petals, as by a drift of snow."

Unlike many of the favourite flowers of Japan, which are only grown in certain districts, and might bloom altogether unobserved if one did not make a special search for them, the cherry is so lavishly planted throughout the Empire that it would be impossible to find any part of the country without some display of the blossom.

The full beauty of the cherry is short-lived, and, almost before one has realised the transformation of the whole landscape, brought about by this wonderful flower, with the help of the glorious April sunshine, a heavy rain-shower or sudden squall will scatter the petals like snow before the wind, and nothing will remain but the young brown leaves and the carpet of fallen petals beneath the trees. We are told of Fujiwara-no-Narinori, of the twelfth century, who prayed to the god Taizanfukun for the prolongation of the glory of his beloved cherry blossom. Fujiwara had planted over a hundred of the trees in his garden, and had, on that account, been named Sakura Machi by the people. It is said that the gods answered his prayer, and allowed the trees to remain in flower for twenty-one days.

Another legend tells of Minamoto-no-Yoshiyo the warrior, who was despatched to fight with Abe-no-Sadato of Oshu. While on his way to the enemy's camp, he passed through groves of falling cherry blossoms, and was struck with lamentation over the changing of nature. His poem remains to this day, and after his death a monument was erected to his memory, on the spot where his inspiration seized him.

It is difficult to decide in which surroundings the cherry blossom shows to best advantage. In the groves or orchards devoted entirely to the *sakura*, where the flower-laden trees will surround one on all sides, there will be cherry blossom, and nothing but cherry blossom almost as far as the eye can reach. From every tree will hang rosy-red lanterns, or a poetical name and inscription will flutter in the breeze, while crowds of visitors wander through the grounds; children clapping their chubby hands in sheer enjoyment of the blossoms, tumbling, in their haste to find fresh treasures, over their gay-coloured kimonos, which, with their gorgeous obi, have been put on to-day for the first time in the honour of spring, and the *sakura*. Perhaps you might prefer to see the trees in a setting of red-brown maples and deep-green pines, in a wilder and more natural state, where one of the many fast-flowing rivers will hurry along beneath the over-hanging boughs, carrying away great drifts of fallen petals; or, again, by the sea-shore, where a few great trees, high up on the cliffs, away from all danger of salt sprays, will make a glorious foreground for the rugged coast-line and the wide stretch of sea beyond. But surely there is no more beautiful setting for the trees than the old temple buildings, with their wooden structures toned by countless ages. A great weeping cherry-tree will stand as a sentinel at the gateway, or a little tree laden with rosy blossoms will guard a tiny shrine.

All through the bright spring days, thousands of sight-seers will climb the stone steps of the temple of Kyomizu—or Good Water—in Kyoto, and

A BUDDHIST SHRINE.

wander through the buildings to the woods beyond. From the terrace they gaze down upon the grove of cherry and maple trees in the valley below, and then away over the grey roofs of Kyoto and the plain beyond, to Osaka, hidden in the morning mists, or to Arashiyama, whose groves will assuredly be visited in due time by these untiring holiday-makers. At every turn a new beauty wipes out the remembrance of the last, and fills our soul with sadness, that nature will not stand still for awhile and give us leisure to enjoy what we know will be here to-day and gone to-morrow. Already the early single flowers are fading and falling ; every gentle breath of wind sends a fresh shower of the thin transparent petals to the ground. To-morrow the heavy clusters of the double pink blossoms will have lost their freshness, and will be hiding their glories under the brown leaves that seem to unfurl and grow while we look at them. Last, and perhaps best of all, will come the double white blossom, whose buds are now hanging in pink clusters, and whose beauty will linger until the close of the "cherry month."

Maruyama Park in Kyoto has a great display of cherry blossom; an enormous drooping cherry of great age, which has taken its name of *Gion sakura* from the Gion temple adjoining, stands in the middle of the park, and thousands of people come to gaze at it every year when it is in flower. Towards the end of March, the park, which has been bleak and deserted all the winter, becomes a scene of bustle and activity. Temporary tea-houses are put up on every available space, hung with innumerable lanterns, and gaily-coloured curtains, most of these being painted with some representation of the cherry blossom. With the unerring taste of the Japanese all the colouring is in harmony with the blossoms, no false note will clash or take away from the beauty of the surroundings. By the 1st of April all is in readiness for the visitors, who from that day onwards will not fail to arrive in a never-ending stream during the whole month. Even if there come days when the rain descends in pitiless torrents, it does not seem to damp their ardour; their clogs may be an inch or so higher; their kimonos will be girt tighter about their knees, to keep them from the mud; each one will carry a huge paper umbrella, black and red, deep blue or purple, or, commonest of all, the natural yellowish colour of the oiled paper, with the owner's name or the sign of the inn to which it may belong in large Katahana characters. Or should it be a late season

THE FEAST OF THE CHERRY BLOSSOMS

and the cherry not be in flower so early, it makes
no difference, still the people come, it is the time
when it *ought* to be in flower, and such is the
imagination in the minds of these curious people,
that they will gaze for hours at a tree with scarcely
more than a tinge of colour in the buds with as
much pleasure as if the tree were in all the glory of
its full flower. On a holiday afternoon, when the
weather is fine, every seat in the tea-houses is taken
up by the pleasure parties, while in the open spaces
the people spread mats brought with them for the
purpose, and sit unfolding those neat little boxes
and packets which contain their mysterious and
wonderful food so unpalatable to our foreign ideas.
Even the cakes and sugar-plums that accompany
the cups of tea, unceasingly supplied by the tired
little *ne sans* of the tea-houses, are in the shape of
cherries impaled on wooden skewers, and eaten with
relish by young and old alike. In no other country
but Japan, where humanity is so closely associated
with nature, and where the people mingle harmoniously with the background of flowers and trees,
could one find such a scene—the entire population
of a great city given up to the whole-hearted
enjoyment of nature.

At nightfall the lanterns are lighted, and flaring

torches round the giant tree cast their lurid light upon the heavily laden branches, which might well belong to some forest tree bending under the weight of freshly fallen snow. Those who cannot leave their work during the day, come forth at night to swell the throng. The sounds of music and feasting, the beating of tom-toms, and the ceaseless dragging of ten thousand clogs mingle with the cries of the toy-seller whose stock of those wonderful paper butterflies, and of the miniature lanterns with the candles ready lit, has to be constantly replenished to supply his endless customers. Thousands of country people, wearied with their round of sight-seeing, spend the night on the grass, only to start again at daybreak on a fresh pilgrimage of innocent pleasure.

The Emperor Kameyama in the twelfth century planted a number of cherry-trees from Yoshino at Arashiyama, a picturesque gorge where the river Katsura, celebrated for the beauty of its rapids, running through a narrow valley, becomes a wide and shallow river and is renamed the *Oi gawa*. Here it is said this Emperor built a pavilion, and, during the cherry month, the Court held high revel for many years. The pavilion has long since disappeared, perhaps swept away by one of the numerous floods which devastate these valleys: but the cherry-trees remain, and here, instead of the stately Court of ancient days, the modern Kyoto sight-seers hold their revels, for Arashiyama may be said to rank first among their favourite spring resorts. They gather in the tea-houses and flower-booths on the banks of the river, and spend their flower-viewing days by the running water and the clouds of white blossom, exclaiming possibly in the words of their poet, "Not second to Yoshino is Arashiyama, where the white spray of the torrent sprinkles the cherry blossom." Barge after barge, roofed over, with matted floor and decorated with innumerable lanterns to suggest a miniature tea-house, will take its load of visitors across the river, or they will spend some hours drifting idly down the stream, eating their midday meal or playing some childish game. Occasionally a flower-laden boat, which has successfully accomplished the passage of the rapids, will come into sight, and the sound of samisens, the saddest of all music, comes floating through the air.

The habit of drinking *saké* while viewing the cherry blossom appears to have originated in the days of the Emperor Richiu, in the fifth century.

While feasting with his courtiers in a pleasure-boat on a lake in one of the royal parks, some petals fell into his wine-cup, and drew the attention of the monarch to the hitherto despised blossom, and he exclaimed, "Without wine, who can properly enjoy the sight of the cherry blossoms?" —a sentiment which appears to have survived to this day. It was not, however, until the eighth century that the cherry blossom rose to the distinction of a national flower. The Emperor Shomu, while hunting on Mount Mikasa, in the province of Yamato, was so struck by the beauty of the blossoms, that he sent some branches, accompanied by some verses of his own writing, to his consort Komio Kogo. Afterwards, in order to satisfy the curiosity of the Court ladies, who had never seen this wonderful flower, he commanded a number of the trees to be planted round the Palace of Nara, whence arose the custom of planting them near all the royal palaces in the country.

The province of Yamato is especially celebrated for its cherry groves, and justly so, as the little mountain village of Yoshino has given the name to the most famous of all the varieties, and has even been called the headquarters of the cherry blossom; and so profuse is the mass of blossom that the poets have compared it to mist or snow upon the hills. The little street of the village winds away up the spur of the hill, past many temples and shrines, until it becomes nothing but the rough stony path which ascends Mount Omine. Although the village stands high above the sea, its own especial kind of cherry is rather an early one; the blossoms are large and single, pale pink in colour; but its beauty is fleeting, and the visitor must go early in the "cherry month" to Yoshino, or he will be greeted by great showers of the falling petals being swirled away on the wind to join the light fleecy clouds on Mount Omine, or down to the mists which hang in the valley below, and nothing will be left but the remains of departed glories. During the few days, early in April, when the blossom is at its best, thousands of pilgrims visit the little village and occupy every available lodging; but the traveller who is not discouraged by the discomfort of primitive Japanese inns, or by the long tedious journey over the mountains from Nara, will find ample reward in the beauty of his surroundings. Mr. Parsons, in his *Notes on Japan*, thus described Yoshino :—

Everything in Yoshino is redolent of the cherry: the pink and white cakes brought in with the tea are in the shape of its blossoms, and a conventional form of it is painted on every lantern and printed on every scrap of paper in the place. The shops sell preserved cherry flowers for making tea, and visitors to the tea-houses and temples are given maps of the district—or, rather, broad sheets roughly printed in colours, not exactly a map or a picture—on which every cherry grove is depicted in pink. And all this is simply enthusiasm for its beauty and associations; for the trees bear no fruit worthy of the name. . . . I was reminded constantly of a sentence a friend had written in one of my books, "Take pains to encourage the beautiful, for the useful encourages itself." It is difficult for an outsider to determine how much of this is genuine enthusiasm and how much is custom or traditional æstheticism, but it really matters little. That the popular idea of a holiday should be to wander about in the open air, visiting historic places, and gazing at the finest landscapes and the flowers in their due season, indicates a high level of true civilisation, and the custom, if it be only custom, proves the refinement of the people who originated it.

Tokyo and its neighbourhood can lay claim to some of the most beautiful spots for viewing the cherry blossoms. The banks of the river Sumida at Mukojima are lined for miles with an avenue of ancient trees bending almost to the water's edge with the weight of their double blossoms. This is the favourite resort of the Tokyo holiday-makers, and crowds of pedestrians, carrying their gourds of wine, inaugurate a veritable *Bureiko* (carnival) and fill the booths and the houses which are

THE PINK CHERRY

CHERRY BLOSSOM

temporarily erected along the banks of the river. Those citizens who can afford the greater luxury of a barge or roofed pleasure-boat spend the evening more peacefully in floating upon the calm surface of the river, gazing at the blossoming trees, cheered by the singing of the geishas and the playing of the samisens. So great is the attraction of cherry blossoms seen by the light of the pale moon, that they have even been given the special name of Yozakura or night cherry flowers. To the foreigner wishing to enjoy the prospect of the cherry blossoms in peace, such boisterous feasting will seem out of harmony with the natural quiet beauty of the spot, and he will do well to turn his steps and to spend a few hours in undisturbed enjoyment of the more dignified setting of Uyeno Park, where the giant trees of single and drooping blossom stand out in splendid contrast to the pines and cryptomerias surrounding the tombs of the Shoguns. Ralph Adams Cram thus describes the scene:—

Here the cherry trees are huge and immemorial, gnarled and rugged, but clutching sunrise clouds caught by the covetous hands of black branches, and held dancing and fluttering against the misty blue of the sky. Here and there a weeping cherry holds down its prize of pink vapour, until it almost brushes the heads of those who pass; here and

there the background of bronze cryptomeria is flecked with
puffs of pink, as though now and then the captive clouds
had burst from the holding of crabbed branches only to be
caught in their escape toward the upper air and prisoned
by the tenacious fingers of the cedar.

At the end of the road the path blurs in odorous mist,
and in a moment we are enveloped in the rosy clouds. As
far as the eye can reach stretches the low-hung canopy of
the thin petals; the trunks of the trees are small and gray,
and one forgets them, or never thinks to associate them with
the mist of pale vapour overhead, hung in the soft air,
impalpable, evanescent, a gauzy cloud, lifted at dawn and
poised breathless close over the earth.

A little wind ripples above, and the air trembles with a
snow of pink petals swerving and sliding down to the carpet
of thin fallen blossoms, while darting children in scarlet and
saffron and lavender crow and chatter, catching at the rosy
flakes with brown fingers.

The light here is pale and pearly as it filters through the
sky of opal blossoms, and it transmutes the small dusky
people into the semblance of butterflies and birds, now
gathering into glimmering swarms of flickering colour, now
darting off with shrieks of delight over the carpet of fallen
petals. Here a slim girl with ivory skin has thrown off her
ivory kimono, and clothed only in a clinging gown of
vermilion crepe opening low on her bosom, barefooted, a
great dancing butterfly of purple rice paper clinging to her
black hair, is swaying rhythmically in an ecstatic dance,
pausing now and then to flutter away like a red bird up the
shadowy slope, until her flaming gown gleams among stone
lanterns half lost in the gloom of great trees. Here a ring
of shrieking children, wrinkled old women, and half-naked
coolies are circling hand in hand in some absurd little game;
and here, there, and everywhere whole families are clustered

on red blankets, eating endless rice and drinking illimitable *saké*, while the tinkle of the samisen is in the air, and strange cool voices sing wistful songs in a haunting minor key. It is a kaleidoscope of flickering colour, a transformation scene of pearl and amber, opal and vermilion.

Koganai, a day's excursion from Tokyo, is another attractive spot in the cherry blossom season—an avenue of double cherry-trees stretching for two and a half miles along the river Tama. As the name suggests, *tama* meaning pearl, the water is clear, and the stream provides the people of Tokyo with their drinking water, which is brought to the city by means of an aqueduct. It is said that some ten thousand trees were originally brought from Yoshino, by command of the Shogun Yoshimune, and planted along the banks of the aqueduct, with the pretty idea that the purity of the blossoms would keep off impurities from the water-supply. Of this vast number of trees, even if they ever really existed, only a few hundreds remain to-day, but sufficient to keep up their old reputation and attract enough visitors for yet another merry and boisterous flower carnival; in fact, throughout the land, wherever there are cherry-trees, during the month of their glory there will be feasting. The blossom seems to act as a magnet to draw the people together, and often by the wayside I have seen just one solitary tree, in all the fulness of its beauty, made sufficient excuse for a miniature feast. Just a few lanterns will be hung in the tree, a few matted benches will be spread out, and an old *Kami san* will be waiting to greet any passing traveller with her cries of *Irasshai—o kake nasai*—Welcome—please sit down, —and the offer of the inevitable tea, tobacco-box, and *hibachi*.

The Emperor Saga, as early as the ninth century, inaugurated the Imperial garden parties to view the cherry blossom, which still take place annually at the old summer palace of the Shoguns, Shiba Rikyu. The gatherings were attended by the writers and poets of the day, who composed odes on the blossoms. Although robbed of many picturesque features by the lamentable custom of wearing foreign dress at Court, these functions are still of great interest to the foreigner, as affording him the only available opportunity of visiting any of the Imperial gardens of the capital.

In spite of the fact that the beauties of Tokyo are fast disappearing—her moats bordered by splendid pines are almost things of the past; broad streets with tramways, brick and stone houses, are

CHERRY-TREE AT KYOMIDZU

fast replacing the narrow streets and little wooden houses of old Yedo; the *Yashiki* or Daimios' houses and gardens are gone, replaced by foreign houses,— Tokyo still retains her cherry-trees. No modern reformer has ever dared to sweep away her avenues of *sakura*, for to the Japanese the cherry is something more than an ordinary flower; it is difficult, if not impossible, for our Western minds to enter into their conception of it. To them the soul of the *sakura*, or cherry blossom, is the soul of Bushido (Chivalry), and the heart of Bushido is the heart of Japan. One of their songs says—

>Hana wa sakura yo,
>Hito wa bushi.
>(Among flowers the cherry,
>Among men the samurai.)

The precepts of Chivalry were started first as the glory of the *élite*, but grew in time to be the aspiration of the whole nation, and they found their ideal in the *sakura*. The phrase, *Chitte koso sakura nari*, meaning "It's a cherry blossom, it falls when it must," was taught in the old feudal days—how to die from loyalty as the cherry blossom, —the ethic of Death was the highest. So to this day their ethics remain the same, and Tokyo retains her cherry-trees, which in spring transform the town into a garden of blossom. The poet Bashio sang in his *hokku* poem—

> Hana wo kumo
> Kane wa Uyeno ka
> Asakusa ka.
> (A cloud of flowers!
> Is it the bell from Uyeno
> Or from Asakusa?)

It is true that wherever the clouds of blossom are low they will shut out the prospect in Tokyo, and one is unable to tell whether the bell which sounds from far away is that of Asakusa or Uyeno.

The number of different kinds of cherry-trees seems unlimited; Japanese authorities quote one hundred distinct varieties. The first, and almost the most beautiful, to flower, is the *Ito sakura* or drooping cherry, with pendent branches like a weeping willow, and so-called from *ito*, meaning thread. These trees attain to a great size and make magnificent specimens. Almost at the same time bloom the *Higan sakura*—equinox cherries—with white single flowers or pale pink. Such are most of the trees at Uyeno, of majestic size, planted, it is said, by one of the Tokugawa Regents in imitation of the hills at Yoshino, though Asakusa yama, a hill in the suburbs of Tokyo, is more often spoken of as the *new* Yoshino. The *Ukon sakura*

CHERRY BLOSSOM

is very lovely, with its clusters of pale greenish-yellow double blossoms, but is rather scarce, and a variety known as *Yaye hotoye* has single and double blossoms on one tree,—*yaye* meaning single and *hotoye* double. The Yoshino cherry I have already described; *Hi sakura* has double blossoms, deep crimson in bud, and bright pink when open. There seems to be a never-ending list of these lovely trees, in bewildering variety—early and late kinds, single, semi-double and double, large and small, from pure white through every shade of blush pink to light crimson, and the one beautiful pale yellow blossom, its outer petals just flushed with pink, suggesting the colouring of a tea-rose rather than a cherry blossom. The double varieties of course bear no fruit, but even the single "equinox cherries" bear none, so the Japanese are satisfied with their splendid blossom and do not worry about the poor insipid little fruit, which is all a cherry represents to them; but they will salt the leaves and drink cherry-flavoured tea under the pink canopy of flowers during the time of the cherry blossoms, when, in the gladness of spring, all the world is making merry.

CHAPTER X

WISTARIA AND PÆONY

THE last petals of the cherry blossoms have only just fallen, and Nature hastens to provide a new treasure for the flower kingdom, and the first blooms of the wistaria *Fuji no hana* will be opening at the base of the quickly growing racemes. Not the far-famed *Wistaria multijuga*, whose immense long sprays of delicate mauve flowers are so associated throughout the world with the name of Japan, but the early-flowering wistaria, *Brachy botris*, with its tufts of white blossoms completely covering the closely pruned branches before any trace of a leaf appears. It would seem as if this modest white wistaria had been allowed by nature to bloom so early, for fear she should be overlooked and not appreciated when her more showy successor flings her purple mantle over the land. The Royal Fuji, fancifully called *Niki-so*, meaning "plant of the two seasons," because, appearing between the third and fourth months (old calendar), it belongs both to spring and summer, has rightly attained her high rank among the floral kingdom of Japan, for in no other country can be seen a restaurant set out for the entertainment of perhaps a hundred guests, who will all feast wrapped in the purple haze of a roof of wistaria blossoms, all from a single vine.

Perhaps the most popular haunt of the pleasure-seeker in the month of May is the celebrated Kameido Temple in Tokyo. Words fail me to describe the beauty of the scene: it is a real feast of *fuji*; the long purple trails cover the large trellises, the wide rustic galleries, and connect the little matted restaurants, where hosts of people throughout the day sit feasting under the purple roof and feeding the gold fish in the lake. The matted benches are set out on a thick mauve carpet of fallen blossoms, and the little maids seem to have a never-ending task in sweeping away great heaps of the freshly fallen flowers, as though fearing that their guests will be smothered by them. No one seems to know so wisely as the Japanese in what surroundings to plant their flowers, so as to show them to their best advantage. Wistaria seems always to be grown near water, so that the trellis which is to bear its flower burden can be built out over the water. So it is at Kameido; and as I sat surrounded, almost smothered, by the blossoms, inhaling their delicious scent and listening to the droning of the bees, I could gaze across the water at the reflection of a never-ending vista of mauve blossoms reaching on one side to the celebrated round wooden bridge, the delight of children, who seemed to cross it in one ceaseless stream, and on the other to the fine old temple, where a few ancient pine-trees are placed just where they will best harmonise with the long purple blossoms. The late sweet-scented white variety will prolong the *fuji* season by a few days; their glory is but short-lived, a few days and then their colour begins to fade, the leaves appear among the blossoms, and their beauty is gone. I felt if I wanted to see wistaria again that year I must fly to the northern provinces, where the bean-scented blossoms will soon be clothing the forest trees. I turned away sadly, not forgetting the Japanese theory that the wistaria loves *saké*. So strong is their belief, that I was told that if you set a jar of the wine under the plant, its spray will grow longer from its desire to reach the jar; so I ordered my

WISTARIA, KAMEIDO

WISTARIA AND PÆONY

little cup of *saké*, sipped it, and then emptied the cup on the roots, according to their custom, hoping that I too might help to contribute to its great size and beauty.

Very lovely is the scene at Kashukabe, where another famous wistaria grows. The vine is said to be some five hundred years old, its pendent clusters over 50 inches long and growing over trellises covering a space of 4000 feet. Noda in the province of Settsu is also celebrated for its wistaria, and a special variety has been named after the place. The cultivation of *Wistaria multijuga*, with its racemes from two to three feet in length, and the individual flowers having a lip of darker purple, seems to belong more especially to the eastern provinces. And it must not be imagined that *all* wistaria in Japan has these immense long sprays. In the whole neighbourhood of Kyoto I know of only two fine specimens of *multijuga*, and all the wild variety seems to be *Wistaria chinensis*, with its tufts of shorter racemes.

Towards the end of the first week in May I made a pilgrimage to see the wistaria blossoms in Kasuga Park at Nara, and I shall never forget the enjoyment of that day, the blessed relief of being able to find a quiet spot away from the gazing crowd, in which to ramble or sit and enjoy the scene. The vines have clambered to the top of many of the tallest pines and cryptomerias, and their blossoms hang in wreaths; in the distance the effect was suggestive of smoke rising among the trees. Many of the lower trees seemed to have been completely taken possession of by the trespasser, and the dead branches transformed into big bouquets of pale mauve. How far more beautiful were these natural supports than the somewhat unsightly bamboo poles which usually form the trellis for the vines. Little glades, down which winds a tiny clear stream, divide the ground, and the banks were covered with these old trees, completely smothered by the weight of blossom. Often the vine seemed not content with covering a single tree, but had thrown out long branches beyond, which, fallen to the ground, had rooted and then risen again to find a fresh prey, thus forming a double arch wreathed with purple tassels. This park is one of the few places in Japan where there is real turf, closely cropped by the herd of deer, and in the open spaces broad stretches of brilliant-coloured *Azalea sinensis* added to the enchantment of the scene and formed a perfect foreground.

To the Japanese mind the *fuji* is essentially feminine, and they find in the wistaria their ideal of woman,—the Japanese woman—whose charm of temperament and whose beauty has been so praised. It is a pretty idea, and it is not difficult to understand their ideal of woman when one observes how the wistaria clings to the undaunted pine, and how gently she falls down, easily moved by a breath of wind and yet firmly holding her own place. The wistaria is regarded as the emblem of gentleness and obedience, and these are the keynotes of a Japanese woman's character.

The young tender leaves of wistaria are sometimes eaten, and also used in the place of tea; and the flowers themselves are used for food in some parts of China. The seeds baked in the fire have very much the same flavour as that of a chestnut. The bark is used for ropes and sandals; and its branches are used, it is said, as cables, and also for bridge-making, as it is supposed that there is nothing more durable than a wistaria bridge. Japanese antiquarians will tell you that in olden times, before carpenters' tools had been invented, the dwellings of the people in Japan were constructed of young trees with the bark left on, fastened together with ropes made of the tough shoots of wistaria, and thatched with the grass called *kava*. *Fuji* appears to be a real Japanese flower, though in the Western countries it is called wistaria, in honour of Caspar Wistar, an American physician.

One of the most celebrated classical *No* dances of Japan has wistaria as its theme. The little square boxes in front of the stage, with its long gallery or bridge (along which the *No* actors make their entrances and exits), are filled by the audience, apparently patiently waiting in quiet, somewhat sleepy expectancy. The long piercing sound of flutes mingled with the curiously sad rhythm of *Tsuzumi* drums has ceased; and the high distinct declamation of the libretto begins. The priest, who is a necessary part of any *No* dance, is the first to appear on the stage; he is supposed to reach Taka no Ura in the province of Ecchu, a place famous for wistaria, and here he meets a country girl who in a short time will reappear as the spirit of the wistaria; she entreats him to pray for her, so that through the virtue of his prayer her flower spirit may enter into Nirvana or Paradise; doubtless the spirit of the last flower of spring is not able to release herself from the world to attain Buddhistic perfection, so she hates to say her quick

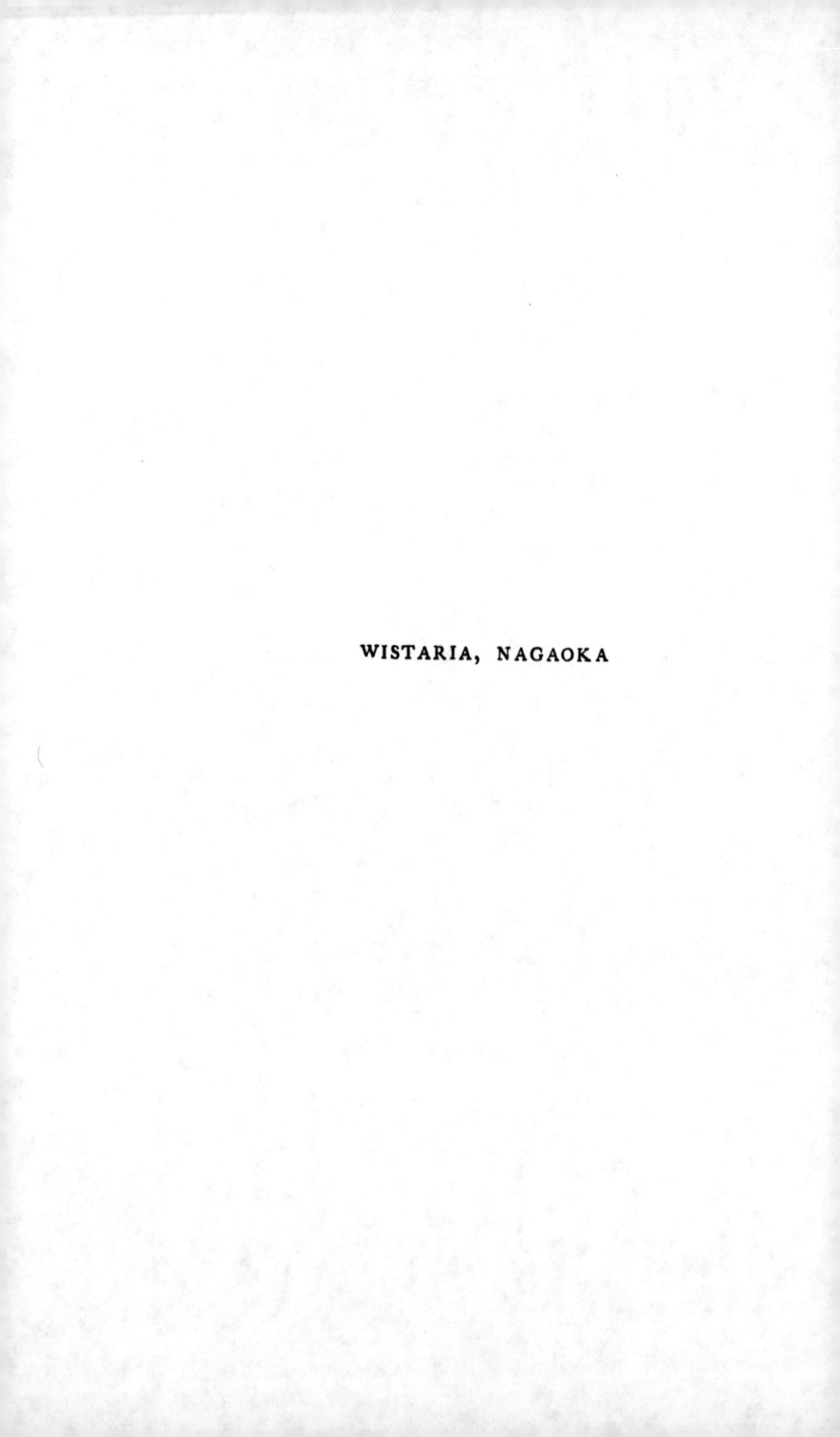
WISTARIA, NAGAOKA

farewell to spring, Presently the flower spirit, arrayed in gorgeous purple brocade, dances her last spring dance, and then, after receiving the priest's repeated prayer, she will disappear with joy. So ends the *No* play, so full of emblematical meaning to the minds of the Japanese.

The wistaria and pæony seem to be closely associated, as not only do they flower at the same time and many gardens seem devoted to their combined culture, but just as in Japanese literature the wistaria is an emblem of womanhood, so in Chinese literature the pæony is compared to a beautiful woman. The pæony seems to be a plant of Chinese origin, and though it can hardly be classed as one of the most popular flowers of Japan, it plays an important part in the art of the country. The tree pæony is a delicate plant and requires scrupulous care and nursing in order that its blooms should attain their full size and colour. It is regarded as essentially the rich man's flower, and therefore it is often called the "flower of prosperity"; another fancy name by which it is known is the "plant of twenty days," because it will preserve its freshness and beauty for that time. The celebrated garden at Honjo in Tokyo combines the cultivation of *botan* (tree pæony) with that of wistaria. A fine old vine of *multijuga* overhangs the pond; but one of the especial features of the garden is the cultivation of wistarias in pots and tubs—some grand old plants, flowering as though they would flower themselves to death. Others there were of all sizes and shapes; some bent and leaning, some bearing veritable canopies of blossoms; some pure white, some the pale mauve *sinensis*, and others the deeper-coloured *multijuga*.

My first visit to "view the pæonies" was rather a disappointment to me, as, in order to protect the blooms from heavy rain or wind storms, the plants are all placed under the cover of temporary matting sheds. They seemed mostly to be grown in pots, and the effect of these rows of plants, each with its large and heavy blossoms supported by bamboo stakes, was somewhat stiff and prim. A few stray plants there were, which, possibly for some slight defect in the shape or colour of the blooms, had not been included in the show collection; and to the uninitiated these gave most pleasure, left standing in the open, their colour blending harmoniously with that of the wistaria blossoms. The pæony gardens seemed no haunt for the holiday-maker, but rather for the serious-minded gardener, who, truly interested in their culture, would spend

A PÆONY GARDEN

hours in quiet contemplation of the plants, discussing the merits of the different varieties with some fellow-enthusiast. There were some hundred different kinds of the tree pæony. The most prized ones were all either pure white blossoms, or those whose colour ranged from pale pink to red,—quite rightly, however rare they may be, the purple-hued and yellow are less valued. Many a private garden belonging to the rich has its pæony show, and the plants are mostly brought from the neighbourhood of Nara, which is celebrated for its pæony gardens. And the gardens at Kabata are also famous for their blooms; where too may be seen the combination of the *fuji* flowers covering long trellises and the little standard trees growing along the margin of the stream, their pendent trails reflected in the water, softening as it were the gorgeous splendour of the flaunting pæony blossoms.

There is no more gorgeous floral sight than the pæony with its tremendous curling petals; but a Japanese artist told me that its fulness in splendour made those with a better poetical fancy and more quiet taste dislike it and think the beauty of the pæony to be even vulgar. Japan is nothing if she be not light and airy, and therefore the Japanese consider flowers with more delicate grace to be more artistic; so the pæony has little chance to become their favourite flower, its beauty is too heavy. It has found, however, some admirers among the poets of Western Japan. In comparison to the people of the eastern provinces the inhabitants of Osaka and Kyoto are said to be more showy in their taste, their art is heavier, so the pæony is called the Western Flower of Japan. If you compare China and Japan, the former's taste in art is more decorative and heavier, and remember what a favourite the pæony is as a decoration for their priceless porcelain. The variety of pæony known as *Pæonia sinensis*, the true Chinese pæony, does not seem to be much regarded in Japan, and little attention seems to be given to its cultivation.

The *botan* calls to mind the pæony lantern, and the pæony lantern or *botan toro* is suggestive of the Buddhist festival of *Bon* (from July 13-16), when the great gates of Hades will open wide, and those dead souls who are still wandering about, being unable to enter Nirvana, will come back again to receive their relatives' prayers, by whose virtue they may get their final rest. So this festival is universally called the Soul Festival: in literature it is closely connected with ghosts. The theatres will all play "ghost plays," as, of course, the story of the pæony lantern is a ghost story.

A beautiful girl called O Tsuyu was the daughter of a certain samurai Ijima San, who lived apart from her father with her faithful maid O Yone. She happened to love Shinzaburo Ogihara, a young samurai, and died of love, and her maid followed her. Ogihara did not know of their death. He observed one summer evening that two young women—who were O Tsuyu and O Yone—passed before the gate of his house, carrying pæony lanterns in their hands, and he welcomed them. During the following seven nights O Tsuyu called on him at night with her usual pæony lantern in hand; and then Shinzaburo was told by his friend that she was not a living person, but a ghost. He appealed to some holy priest to protect him from the ghost. The priest gave him some charm to hang at his door; and when the charm one night was taken away, Ogihara was found dead the next morning.

There is a rather charming ghost story of the pæony which is of Chinese origin; the story is called the Ko Gyoku or Incense Jewel. Kaseikyu of Rozan, of fairy beauty, is famous for its pæonies. In Kaseikyu there lived a young scholar called

Kosei. He was looking out of his window one day, and to his amazement he observed a beautiful young lady dressed in white who stood among the pæonies; he saw her so often that he fell in love with her, and wrote a love-song dedicated to her fair soul. Then she appeared as in a dream to him one day and said, "My name is Ko Gyoku; I was brought here from the city of Heiko, and my life is not without sadness." They promised to love each other, they continued to meet every day, till one day Ko Gyoku told him sadly that she had to go away; and the next morning, strange to say, Kosei observed that the pæonies in the garden had disappeared. Was she not the spirit of one of the pæonies? He passed day and night in sad dreams and with many tears, thinking over his unhappy fate in love. To his surprise Ko Gyoku appeared after a long time, and they held each other's hands, but the man found the lady's hand cold. Ko Gyoku said, "Yesterday I was the living spirit of the flower, but to-day I am merely the ghost. My body is cold, the flower is dead." However, she was to his eyes as beautiful as before. She continued, "If you will be kind enough to give a cupful of water to the roots of

WISTARIA, KABATA

the old pæonies every day, you will receive a reward in due course of time," and disappeared. Kosei found the next morning that new sprouts were beginning to come out from the old roots.

The pæony was introduced into Japan from China in the eighth century, but failed to gain universal popularity, on account of the difficulty of cultivating it successfully ; but the Rich Man's Flower came to be regarded as the king of flowers, and therefore the lion and the peacock, the kings of the animal world, are its companions in art. They are always painted together in the decoration of a temple or palace wall, and when lions dance on the Japanese stage they always have a gorgeous background of pæonies. There may be more of myth than truth in the pretty story of Ichinenko, a kind of pæony, whose flowers turned crimson when Yo Ki Hi (the beloved mistress of the Emperor Genso, famous in Chinese history in connection with the pæony) accidentally touched the petals of the flower with her rouged finger-tips, when she appeared in the garden after finishing her morning toilette.

So strong is the feeling among Japanese poets that the flower is lacking in any poetical grace, that the *Hokku*[1] poet Hyoroku remarks in his Essay on a Hundred Flowers, "The pæony is like the mistress glorified in one's love, who acts as she pleases without any consideration for another's feeling. It has such an attitude, as if it spit out a rainbow into the blue sky." The poet Bushon, who has written more lines on the pæony than any other poet, says—

<blockquote>
Niji wo haite   (Spitting forth a rainbow
Hirakanto suru   Is about to bloom
Botan hana.   The pæony flower.)
</blockquote>

---

[1] *Hokku* is a poem of seventeen syllables.

CHAPTER XI

AZALEAS

EARLY in May the brilliant-coloured azaleas seem determined, by the splendour of their hues, to try and outshine their graceful, tender-coloured predecessors the plum, peach, and cherry. Surely no other plants ever equalled their display of colours—every shade—pure white, cream, salmon, pink, scarlet, orange, and purple; but even all this feast of colour will not make up for the delicate colour of the blossoming trees. There are so many different varieties of azalea, so many different ways of planting them, and even such a variety in their natural growth, that it is hard to say in which surroundings they appealed to me most.

The most celebrated place for "viewing azalea blossoms"—*Satsuki no hana*—in all Japan is in the district of Shinjuku, a suburb of Tokyo, where the show gardens, known as the florists' gardens of

Okubo-mura, present a wealth of colour which I feel powerless to describe. These gardens, or rather azalea plantations, as no other plants are grown, are of very ancient date, and were frequented by the Tokugawa Regents, with whom they were as popular as they are with the sight-seer of to-day. A few sen will suffice to obtain permission to enter a never-ending succession of these little gardens, and so dazzled was I by their splendour that I do not remember that any one seemed more beautiful than another. Imagine these great bushes of immense size and great age simply smothered by their blossoms. Not a leaf was to be seen. My eyes ached at last, and I longed for the repose of a stretch of green. In and out among great banks of the scarlet and crimson *Kaba-renge*, the variety which flowers before the leaves appear,—on past beds of *Azalea indica* with its large double and semi-double blooms of every shade, the paths will lead us, as if through a maze; and surely this mass of colour helps to bewilder one. I was assured one venerable old bush, the thickness of whose stem testified to its great age, bore each year eight thousand blooms; so closely packed did the blossoms appear to be, that it would have been no surprise to me had I been told they numbered eight million instead of

AZALEAS

thousands. The whole district was thronged with holiday-makers visiting the little gardens in one never-ending stream. But one thing differed here from all the other floral feasts I had ever seen in Japan : there were few, if any, little tea-houses set up in the gardens for the entertainment of the guests, who generally sit sipping tea, or some more potent beverage, and gaze upon the especial flower they have perhaps tramped many weary miles to see. Here there was no tea-drinking, they all retreated to the neighbouring restaurants ; and why ? The reason was not far to seek : no human eyes could sit and gaze at that mass of colour for more than a few consecutive moments ; one would leave the garden blinded. The whole air was sweet with their delicious scent; the bees were busy collecting honey, especially from the hearts of the *sinensis* blooms, which seemed the sweetest-smelling variety. No visitor to Japan should miss spending a few hours at Okubo, for surely in no other place in the whole world can such a wealth of colour be seen. The soil near Tokyo must be especially suited to azaleas, as there are many other gardens and parks which in this flower month will be gay with their blossoms.

I have mentioned Okubo first, because it is the

most celebrated place for azaleas, here every variety and colour are collected in one dense mass; but there were many other places where the blossoms gave me more true pleasure, and where I spent many hours enjoying the scene.

At Nagaoka, in the neighbourhood of Kyoto, many a day have I spent, and I know of no place where one can sit more comfortably and peacefully lost in admiration and contemplation. Nagaoka has a large sheet of water, apparently artificial, but beautified by the great bushes of scarlet azalea along the shore, and the great splashes of colour in the water cast by their reflection. Here they are all one variety, with true fiery scarlet blossoms, and as I sat in one of the little thatched houses built out on piles in the water, great bushes were crowding round me; it seemed as though they had even cast their rosy hue upon the houses, as are not all their walls pink, as if they too reflected the colour of the blossoms?

I felt I should like to sleep among the azaleas and see them in the early dawn, and watch the mist clear off the water when the sun's first rays would light up their dazzling splendour. But that could not be. Nagaoka, after all, is only a restaurant, though each party of guests is entertained in a

AZALEAS, NAGAOKA

separate little house. They are frail structures these little houses, with only their paper *shoji* to protect one from the chilliness of the night, and remember, summer is not yet here; all through the month of May there will be a freshness in the air to remind you that spring is not yet gone. So to Kyoto we must return; but there was plenty of consolation to be found there.

The gardens of the old Awata Palace were a blaze of colour, the azaleas lighting up this beautiful old landscape garden, which at other seasons of the year is apt to look grey and cold and uncared for. The garden here is like two separate gardens; the first part, complete in itself, is the work of the great Kobori Enshu, and the second part, where the azaleas are the glory of the garden, is the work of Soami. Standing between the two is a grand old lantern, whose history is listened to with rapt attention by the little knots of sight-seers who are led by the old priest round the garden and up through the bank of azaleas to look over the great town below, with Hiesan rising in the distance.

Many a little temple garden is quite transformed when the azalea bushes are in flower, their little miniature mountain sides are gay with the blossoms; though often the better the gardens are cared for, the fewer the blossoms, as, in order to keep the bushes in their regular and prescribed shapes, the flowers have to be sacrificed. The little garden of Chishaku-in I can recall, as having the brilliant-coloured bushes in pleasing contrast to the subdued tones of the clipped box and juniper-trees, and the greyness of the lichen-covered lanterns and mossy stones. No doubt there were many such little gardens and also private gardens, but the flower month is too short, and one can only visit the most favoured places or where chance happens to lead one's steps.

For those who prefer to enjoy the azaleas in their wilder state, there are many places where they can wander undisturbed and inhale their scent which comes wafted on the breeze. I am thinking now of Kasuga Park at Nara, where great stretches of *Azalea sinensis* form a brilliant foreground for the wistaria-laden trees. Nature seems to have arranged a veritable picture, almost too beautiful to be real. These gorgeous blossoms shade from delicate yellows and pale pink, through to the brightest orange and flame colour, growing as the woodland scrub. They are not more than a few feet in height, possibly their growth has been stunted by the deer; but they form in places a real carpet or clothe the

AZALEAS, AWATA

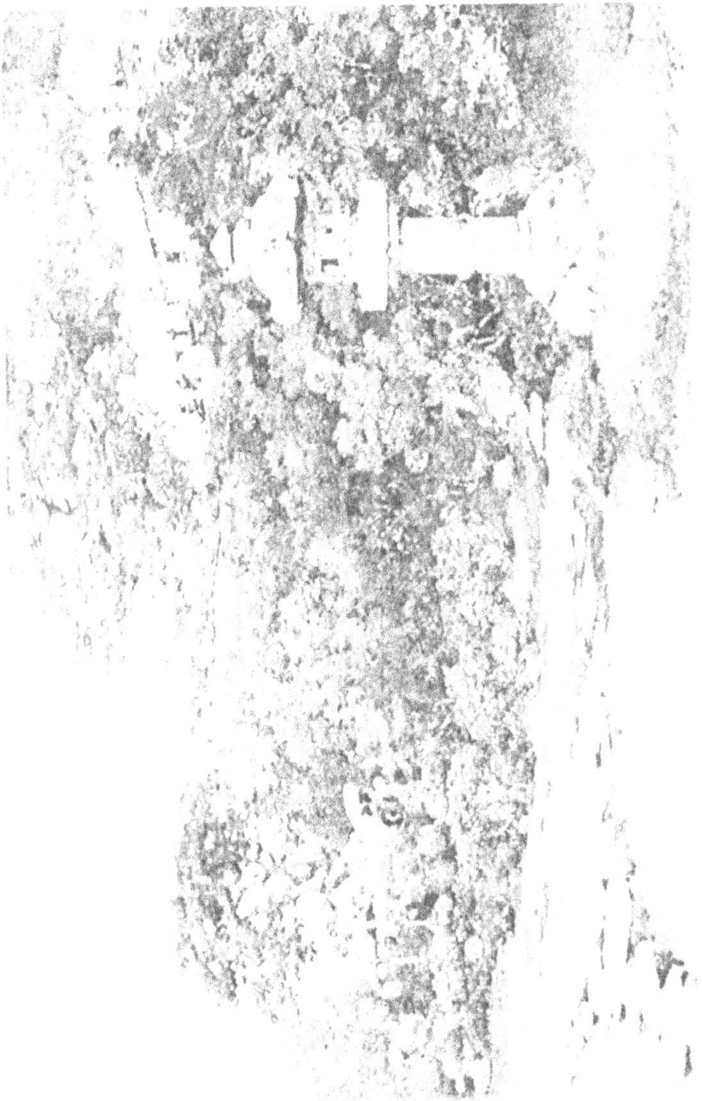

banks of the little streams, their colour vying with the splendour of the great temple beyond.

I had heard so much of the beauty of the cherry blossom and wistaria and the glory of the maples, and their fame is amply justified; but no one had told me of the beauty of the azaleas, and never had I realised how essentially they belong to Japan. Throughout the length and breadth of the land they seem to grow, and there appeared to be few places where one variety or another had not found a home. Their pale purple blossoms were hanging from the cliffs among the white-flowered andromeda bushes late in April, when I paid a flying visit to Miyajima, and a few days later I found them again on the banks of the canal on my way from Otsu. In the country round Hikone the more brilliant-coloured forms had found a home, and under the old pine-trees, broken here and there by a rocky projection, or even a few grey tombstones of some long-forgotten graveyard, the banks were covered with an undergrowth of azaleas. Farther north the railway leading to Aomori will wind its way through country which at all seasons of the year is beautiful, but how far more beautiful when the salmon-pink low-growing azalea forms an undergrowth to the pine woods; wherever the trees have been thinned the rocky ravines are all lighted up with their colour. The azaleas at Nikko and Chuzenji have been described elsewhere, and I feel as if all the country during those short weeks will "always be seen in my mind through a rosy hue of azalea blossoms."

CHAPTER XII

THE IRIS

IF I were to be asked which of all the show gardens in Japan—a garden devoted to the cultivation of one especial flower—gave me most pleasure to visit, I should unhesitatingly answer Hori-kiri, the garden of *hana shobu* or *Iris Kaempferi*, in the neighbourhood of Tokyo. Throughout the month of June this garden remains a feast of subdued colour; for the iris is no gaudy, flaunting flower, but a delicate blossom shading from pure white, through every shade of mauve and lilac to rosy purple, and so deep a blue as to be almost black. In the first days of June the paths winding through the rice fields from the banks of the river Sumida will be crowded with sight-seers whose steps are all bent in one direction and with the same intent —to pay their annual visit to Hori-kiri; and throughout the month this never-ending stream continues from early dawn until the setting of the sun or the rising of the moon. Flower-sellers there will be too, one perhaps with only a modest bunch of half-opened buds in a wooden tub shaded from the sun by a large umbrella, not the unpicturesque object recalled to our English minds by the word umbrella, but one made of pale yellow paper, large and flat, with bamboo ribs, the owner's name inscribed in bold, black Chinese characters—or farther on a little stall decked with lanterns, and a gay-coloured curtain with some device suggestive of the iris; tiny toys, little fairy baskets of split bamboo with just one iris blossom, or fans painted with a giant bloom covering the whole fan, and other dainty trifles, to carry home to the little ones left at home or as a souvenir of this iris-land.

The garden of Hori-kiri must be of very ancient date, as the fine old pine-trees, dwarfed and gnarled maple and juniper bushes, are not the growth of this generation, or even the last. The garden is said to date from some three centuries, and to be handed down from father to son, always in the same family. Nothing could be more perfectly laid out for the proper display of its especial flower, the shaping of the beds, the placing of the bridges, and even the colouring of the little summer-houses in which to entertain their host of guests—all has been thought out by this artistic family; and last, but by no means least, the clothing of the little maids who wait on them with untiring zeal—their kimonos and obis all harmonising in colour.

I have lingered too long on the surroundings of the flowers, and the reader will want to know more of this wonderful flower which deserves so much attention—it does indeed deserve the attention, for surely by the middle of the "dew month" it is hard to imagine anything more beautiful than the scene which meets the eye. Some seventy varieties of this king of irises are grown, many raised from seed and jealously treasured by the owner of the garden. There are early and late varieties, three weeks almost between their time of flowering, but by the second week in June the second blooms of the early varieties will have opened and the first blooms of the later ones, so the effect is as if all were flowering together; every shoot of the plants seems to bloom; there are no gaps in their serried ranks. The mere variety is amazing. Some are pure white, only veined with a faint tinge of green; some have a margin of lilac; some are shaded; some mottled;

but surely the most beautiful of all is just a great single bloom of one shade, be it white, lilac, or blue. Many people prefer the duplex flowers with an inner row of small petals, but to me this form seemed to have lost some of the natural beauty and grace of the true iris. I tried to learn something of their cultivation, hoping it might be of help to those who grow those poor specimens known in England as *Iris Kaempferi*. It is not the plants themselves, or the varieties, which are at fault, for many thousands of roots leave the Hori-kiri garden every year to be scattered throughout the world,—it would seem to be the soil and climate which they resent and stubbornly refuse to adopt; for a few years they linger and even bravely flower, and then they begin to pine and droop like some poor home-sick mortal pining for his native land.

August appears to be the especial month for dividing the roots or replanting them, so that month had better be chosen as the beginning of the iris year. The yellowing foliage is ruthlessly cut to half its natural height and the plants divided, for no clump is ever allowed to grow so large and old that it is hollow in the centre; the outer shoots appear to be the strongest, and have most promise of bloom for the following year. The beds are

AN IRIS GARDEN

THE IRIS

sunk a foot or so below the paths; and the rich soil is like a quagmire, not with standing water, but like swampy ground. In November the plants are all cut down, in preparation for the first dressing of manure in December. The liquid sewage is liberally applied, once towards the end of the year, and then again after an interval of a few weeks, the final dressing being given in January. By February the growth has started, and once the young leaves appear there can be no more manuring, or the foliage would suffer. From now until the time of flowering, the regulation of the irrigation seems to be the chief matter to ensure success in their cultivation. Each variety has its own especial name, generally with some poetical meaning, but difficult for the European ear to grasp, and I noticed that, no doubt for the sake of the foreign market, all the rows were numbered as well as named.

Do not imagine that this is the only iris garden of Japan. There are many others, though I always think that Hori-kiri ranks first, not only for the beauty of the garden, but the actual flowers seem larger and better grown than anywhere else. Only a few minutes' drive from Hori-kiri will take you to Yoshino-en, celebrated for its wistaria as well as its irises. The ground is larger than Hori-kiri and the irises are well grown, but as the garden is not devoted entirely to their culture the effect is not so pleasing. The whole district almost seemed devoted to the culture of *shobu*—many, many fields of them I passed; but as they are grown entirely for the sake of cutting the blooms for market, there is never any mass of colour to be seen.

The gardens at Kabata, belonging to the Yokohama Nursery Company, are perhaps the most extensive iris gardens in Japan; I felt almost dazzled and bewildered by the very size of the grounds—acres of irises—a beautiful sight; but I never derived the same pleasure from it as from the smaller garden. The iris is one of the few flowers which seems to be allowed to enter into the precincts of a true Japanese landscape garden: in many a private garden a stream will be diverted to feed an iris bed, placed where a piece of swampy ground would be most in keeping with the rest of the miniature landscape; or even the margin of a tiny lake will be utilised for just a few plants of *shobu*. I remember seeing an old priest tending his little colony of irises, which no doubt were chosen with great deliberation from a large collec-

THE IRIS

tion for some especial beauty. How often have I seen an old man and woman considering on which particular favourite their few sen shall be expended, and then departing, the happy possessor of a new treasure to add to their little store. My friend the priest's collection all grew in pots; they did not look as though they would attain their full height and beauty; but as if to reward the loving care bestowed on them they all showed promise of flower; and no doubt in due time they will have been arranged so as to give the best effect and greatest pleasure to their grower.

I asked a Japanese who, with his little gentle wife, was sitting in quiet contemplation and evident enjoyment of the scene, to tell me something of the flower as it appeals to the Japanese, and he said: "We live here in the choicest floral kingdom; and to our mind the flowers are beautiful, and we do not ask why or how, the sight of their beauty is far more real to us than any meaning which they may suggest. You will find no other nation like Japan, which loves Nature so truly in her varied forms and holds communion with all her aspects; we love the iris as a flower, but as nothing else. I cannot make my mind associate it with any meaning of zeal or chivalry, nor do I think of it as any messenger; it appeals to me only as a little quiet beauty of the water side, making friends with the sadness of the rainy season. In our poems the iris is almost inseparable from water; one of our celebrated poetesses has written the following seventeen-syllable poem—

> Midzu ga kaki,
> Midzu ga kashikeri
> kakitsubata.
>
> (Water was the painter,
> Water again was the eraser
> Of the beautiful fleur-de-lis.)

"It is the universal custom throughout Japan to celebrate the fifth day of May by hanging bunches of *shobu* beneath the eaves of our houses, and to put them into the hot water of the public baths, as it is perfectly delicious for the bathers to inhale their odour. We also drink *saké* in which they have been steeped, on the same day. I felt proud to hear that the fleur-de-lis, as I believe you call the iris, is the national flower of France, as I like to think that it has found a home in the West, and when I was told that the flower which was put above Solomon's greatest glory was not the lily of our country, but that of the iris family, I felt glad and agreed with it."

THE IRIS

The delicate *Iris Tectorum* would be an immense addition to our English flower gardens, if only our summers were hot enough to bake their roots sufficiently to make them flower. I succeeded in making them grow; they threw up their shoots each year, but never one single flower, until at last, disgusted, I condemned them, like so many other treasures brought from foreign climes, as unsuited to our cold grey skies. Late in May these irises will be in full bloom and forming a purple spur on the top of the thatched straw roofs of the farmhouses; they are generally planted in this way (hence their name), and transform the roof ridge of many a peasant's dwelling into the aspect of a flower garden. Many different reasons are ascribed to their being planted in this manner; some say the irises are planted to avert the evil spirits, and there is a superstition that they are efficacious in the prevention of disease. There is also a legend that during one of the famines that devastated the land in olden days an order went forth that all cultivated land was to be given up to the growing of rice, but that the women of Japan, determined to save their iris roots, from which their powder (so essential to the toilette of every young Japanese lady) is made, planted them on the roofs of their houses. I give the tale with all due reserve, as I was never able to verify it, nor do I even know for certain that their precious *shiroi* is made from iris roots.

> Other people no less positively affirm the growth to be accidental. Others, again, assert that the object is to strengthen the thatch. We incline to this latter view; bulbs do not fly through the air, neither is it likely that bulbs should be contained in the sods put on the top of *all* the houses in a village. We have noticed, furthermore, that in the absence of such sods, brackets of strong shingling are employed, so that it is safe to assume that the two are intended to serve the same purpose. (Chamberlain's *Things Japanese*.)

No matter the reason for their being so planted—be it for protection, be it for the sake of vanity or merely for safety—the effect is none the less charming, and later in the year these little roof gardens are sometimes gay with *Hemerocallis aurantiaca* or a stray tuft of scarlet Nerine.

The true *Iris japonica* or *chinensis* is a shade-loving plant, with many lavender-coloured flowers on a branching stem, each outer petal marked with purple lines, and in the centre of the flower a deep orange horn. Like so many delicately marked flowers, it has a very short life, each individual bloom appearing to last only from one

IRISES

sunrise to the next, but the stems bear so many blooms that other buds quickly open and fill the gap of yesterday's blossom.

Iris gracilipes seems the commonest and most free-flowering of all the irises. In May its graceful purple flowers and vivid green grass-like foliage seemed to fringe each pond, and the only fault I had to find with this form of iris was the short duration of its flowering season; the plants bloom so freely they appeared to flower themselves to death, and after one short week their slender heads would hide themselves until the resurrection of the next "flower month."

I learnt that the *Iris lævigata*, which appears to be synonymous with Kämpfer's iris, is much used as a decoration for ceremonies and congratulatory occasions, but on account of its purple colour it is not desirable for weddings, though permissible for betrothals. It is much honoured in the art of flower arrangement, and ranks high among the flowers used for the vase on the *tokonoma*; and the leaves are as much prized as the flowers, lending themselves to the bending and twisting required to attain the regulation curves. As a rule it is not permissible to use the leaves alone of a plant which may bear a flower, or the flowerless branches of a shrub which may bear blossoms or berries; but *Iris japonica* seems an exception to this rule, and the leaves alone may be used before the flowers appear. The first of the ten artistic virtues attributed to certain special combinations is headed in Mr. Conder's list by *Simplicity*—expressed by rushes and irises in a two-storey bamboo vase. The beautiful arrangement known as *Rikkwa* (double stump arrangement) consists of a combination of pine, iris, and bamboo grass.

CHAPTER XIII

THE MORNING GLORY

"*ASAGAO* blooms and fades so quickly, only to prepare for the morrow's glory," such is the theme of one of the oldest songs on the *asagao* or morning glory, written by the Chinese priest at the temple of Obaku near Uji, who is said to have been the first person to introduce the flower to Japan.

It was but a primitive weed when it first came from China; it is only in the land of its adoption that it has evolved its thousand varying forms and developed into the floral wonder of to-day. It was still a semi-barbarous beauty, and had not advanced to its present plane, when *Kaga no Chiyo* wrote her well-known morning glory poem, better known to us from Sir Edwin Arnold's version—

> The Morning Glory,
> Her leaves and bells have bound
> My bucket handle round;

> I could not break the bands
> Of those soft hands.
> The bucket and the well to her I left;
> "Lend me some water, for I come bereft."

For centuries the *asagao* in Japan remained the same trifling little Chinese flower, only the wild morning glory of the bamboo fences in the back gardens; but even then the bright poetesses of the Kyoto Court admired it, and the Nara poets sang its praises. As they delighted to write of the fleeting condition of our human lives, they found a congenial subject in the morning glory, for it is true that no flower has a briefer life and beauty, and the buds of yesterday are flowers to-day, but only for a few short hours, and then nothing will be left but ruin and decay; though how quickly fresh buds will appear and fresh flowers open to be the morrow's "morning glory."

It was not until the eighteenth century that the *asagao* became fashionable among the Daimyos and *hatamoto*, who worked wonders in its cultivation in the rival *Yashiki* or noblemen's gardens at Yedo. Their blossoms developed in size, depth, and variety of colour, until suddenly at the close of the eighteenth century a spell of cold weather during their season of flowering, dwarfed the blossoms and

THE MORNING GLORY

ruined all the seeds in Yedo. So the *asagao* culture was dropped until the *Tempo* period (1830). Then a revival of interest culminated in the mad craze at the time of Commodore Parry's visit, when princes, priests and potentates, nobles, *hatamoto*, and gardeners all vied with each other in the culture of this flower. Fancy prices were put on plants and seeds, as much as fourteen or eighteen yen (2s.) being given for one seed of some new favourite. Naritaya of Yedo and Tonomura of Osaka were rival gardeners, and the latter sent his precious flowers to the Yedo show by means of relays of coolies, to compete with those grown at Yedo.

The restoration and complete change of social conditions were unfavourable to the culture of the morning glory, as it again went out of fashion and only languished, until its recent revival about fifteen years ago, when an *asagao* club was formed and many prominent persons became members.

To-day the craze has spread among all classes, and there is hardly a house—more especially in Tokyo, but almost throughout the country—where there are not a few pots of this favourite flower, it being within the reach of the poorest in the land; for a few sen the seeds may be procured to raise the plants which are so often grown upon the house-top.

Iriya (an attractive name meaning "Within the Valley"), beyond Uyeno Park, is the most famous place in Japan for the morning glory; here thousands of carefully trained plants of every shade and variety of colour, fancy flowers less than half an inch in size, in clusters, and shaped like a butterfly orchid, and other strange varieties may be seen; some trained in pots over light bamboo frameworks representing rustic structures and other quaintly designed frames. The gardens are visited by hundreds of visitors in the early morning, for it is at four o'clock in the morning of a scorching July or August day that the plants will look their best: the buds will just be opening, the faded flowers of yesterday will have fallen, and all will be fresh and make you forget the heat of the day that is dawning. One of the *asagao* experts remarked to me—

We don't call him an *asagao* man, however large his garden be, however good the other preparations; the rarest *asagao*, one which makes our mouths water, as we say, comes frequently from the hands of a *Hachiko* or *Kumako*, and is often raised upon the roofs in Nihonbashi or Kyobashi, where the ground is too dear for any garden, where we say "one handful of ground means one handful of gold." And there's

THE MORNING GLORY

almost no expense in *asagao* cultivation. What's needed for it is only a little time to spare—the little time which you can spare from the resting hours or nap-time in the midsummer days. And any common sort of pot which you can buy for two or three sen will do just as well. And since it is the glory of early morning you have not to prepare anything, even when you invite your friends; a cup of tea will be sufficient. We hear quite often of cases of chrysanthemum parties which were the cause of poverty; but the *asagao* is not such a vulgar thing at all. And, on the other hand, it will make you forget the summer heat. It is the nature of the flower to love the intense heat; in the hot weather you have them more beautiful. The *asagao* man is simply glad to have the hottest days: "Surely to-morrow morning's display will be a splendour," he will say. He will not lose his time in taking a nap, but busy himself arranging the flower vines; and his brain will not suffer from the heat if he wear a large hat—on the contrary it will feel better. I have seen many cases of *asagao* cultivation curing brain illness. And it represents the true spirit of Japanese democracy; it is such an aristocratic flower, like the chrysanthemum. A peer and a heimin will equally enjoy it: at the Himpivokwai (*asagao* show) people of every station have equal freedom and enjoyment.

CHAPTER XIV

THE LOTUS

THE "time of the lotus" is suggestive of the damp hot August days when from earliest dawn the cicadas will be singing, if their discordant noise can be described as song, and the croaking of the frogs day and night, makes one wonder at last whether frogs *never* grow hoarse, or cicadas *never* tire of singing. From the last weeks in July till the first weeks of September the lotus will be blooming bravely, undaunted by the sun's fierce rays; and the first breath of autumn, which brings new life and energy to a human being after the heat of the summer, will mean death to the lotus. Truly it is a beautiful flower this flower of Buddha, as from its close association with the Buddhist religion it seems essentially to belong to Buddha. The colossal figures known as the Dai butsu at Kamakura and Nara sit in immovable calm as

LOTUS AT KODAIJI

though drawing inspiration from the bronze lotus before them; the silence of their souls is the silence of the flowers, and the shape of the open blooms in the sunlight is the symbol of Buddha's enlightenment. Every little idol of Buddha, be it in the family shrine or grand and stately temple, sits upon a lotus throne; the temples are all decorated with carved lotus or the freshly cut flowers in their season; gold and silver paper lotus are carried at funerals; tombstones are often set upon a stone base in the form of a lotus flower, and lotus beds are planted near shrines. The mighty feudal lord Iyeyasu sleeps in the silence of Nikko's cryptomerias, hearing only once in a while the long sad cry of a great bell, and before him as his only companions are the eternally same bronze lotus flowers. So not only is the lotus the especial flower of Buddha, but it is also regarded as the flower of death, and for that reason it is disliked as a decoration for any occasion of rejoicing.

There is no more beautiful sight than a lotus bed at the dawn of a hot August day. Stately and yet tender is the beauty of the lotus blossom, the great buds opening with a noise which is indescribable to one who has not heard it; and how quickly the delicate pink or white petals unfurl, as though hastening to make the most of their short life, for before the overpowering heat of the August noonday the flower closes, to open once more on the morrow and then die a graceful death; the petals dropping one by one, but still retaining all the freshness of their colour, and then nothing will be left but the great seed pod, very beautiful in itself, but not as beautiful as the great bluish-green leaves studded with dewdrops, which seem to reflect every passing cloud. For the beauty of the lotus lies not only in its flowers; you will begin to see the beauty of the plant even when the tender young leaves peep out shyly upon the surface of a pond in early June; their colour is dark brown, and the Japanese call them *zeniba* from their resemblance to the shape of copper money. Then day by day the leaves will spread and float out as a spirit upon the water, gradually the stalks grow and they will get higher and higher, their broad curling surfaces losing the bronze colour and turning to every shade of soft green and deep emerald; and so through all the scorching summer days they remain fresh and cool to look upon, until in October they begin to flag, but they will be beautiful even in death. The stalks then seem too weak to carry their burden any longer, and suddenly, even as one

LOTUS AT KYOMIDZU

watches them, the stem bends near the top, and the great curling leaf will give one last shiver in the breeze, topple, and turn over and hang with head bent as if in penitence.

Though the beauty of each individual flower may be short-lived, each morning will bring fresh buds, which in a few hours open into fresh flowers, bringing new beauty to the lotus bed; so its glory lasts for six long weeks.

For the true lover of the lotus there can be scarcely any night, for soon after midnight he must rise and start for the lotus pond to see their real beauty and hear the opening of the buds with the sudden touch of dawn; so in old days the Japanese used to visit the famous Shinobazu pond in Uyeno Park, where the little temple dedicated to the goddess Benten stands on a small peninsula, as though to protect the lake from desecration, though if that were her mission she has surely failed. Four years before, I too, in the early morning, had visited the Shinobazu pond, and filled with awe and admiration had spent many hours watching the rosy petals open, and the great glaucous leaves toss hither and thither with every breath of wind, and the iridescent dragon-flies darting through the air; until driven away at last by the overwhelming heat, I had to seek shelter from the sun. Again last August I felt I must see the lotus at Uyeno in all their glory; but I feel ashamed, for the traditions of Japan, to say what greeted me. Great staring Exhibition buildings in the worst possible taste have been built all along the shores of this historical lake. But the worst part is still to come: overshadowing the little shrine and into the very heart of one of the great stretches of lotus leaves dashed a water-chute. It took my breath away. I stood spell-bound, and then turned away with horror and asked myself, as many other people, alas! are asking: "Are the Japanese losing all their artistic feelings?"

Happily there are still many quiet spots where lotus grow, away from the desecrating hand of the "new Japan," and there we can sit and enjoy this "emblem of purity," its clean fresh flowers and leaves rising unsullied from the stagnant mud; and this is one reason for associating it with a religious life, or comparing it to the virtuous soul of a woman who lives in suspicious surroundings.

A favourite Buddhist precept says: "If thou be born in the poor man's hovel, but hast wisdom, then art thou like the lotus flower growing out of the mud!"

THE LOTUS

Wherever undisturbed pools and channels of muddy water exist, the lotus is to be found: the old moats surrounding the remains of a grand old Daimyo's castle, the muddy temple or monastery ponds, and even the ditches beside the railway, will all be rendered gay in the summer, when the great pink and white lotus are in bloom. Their history is a very old one, for their beauty is sung in the old Buddhist *sutra*, and one passage describing the golden glory of Paradise tells of "a pond where the lotus flowers large as a carriage-wheel grow; the green flowers shine in green light, the yellow flowers in yellow light, red flowers in red light, and the white flowers are supreme in beauty and odour."

It may be true that the leaves are as large and round as a carriage-wheel—of a Japanese carriage, a *kuruma*; and certainly I should be afraid to state rashly how large and high the foliage of the white variety may grow. The white *Nelumbium speciosum*, for all the so-called lotus of Japan are really this species of water-lily, has a powerful and sweet perfume; but the pink ones, which are far more beautiful, have but little scent. I think the leaves and their stems, as well as the flower, must have their own peculiar odour; for often I noticed near lotus beds, where no blossoms were to be seen, a strong and rather sickly perfume came floating in the air in whiffs which will always be associated in my mind with lotus, as I cannot compare their scent to that of any other flower.

There are other varieties, one a deep crimson colour and one called "gold-thread lotus," but these are seldom seen. The Indian lotus has a larger double flower, deep pink in colour, which never closes day or night, and the blooms last in beauty for five or six days. In India, the source and centre of Buddhism, the lotus has been chosen as a national flower, and Burmah also is famed for its lotus; so wherever Buddhism makes its presence felt, there you will find the lotus. Sir Monier Williams says that "its constant use as an emblem seems to result from the wheel-like form of the flower—the petals taking the place of spokes, and thus typifying the doctrine of perpetual cycles of existence."

The lotus is a favourite subject with the Japanese artist in conjunction with the mandarin duck and other water-fowl, and so faithfully do the Japanese represent their flowers that each vein in the leaves seems to be depicted if not exaggerated. Mr. Parsons admirably describes the lotus, and also this form of exaggeration and mannerism in their art—

Take for example the spots on the lotus stems; if you look very closely you can see that there are spots, but certainly it could not strike every artist as a marked feature of the plant, for they are not visible three yards away. But some master noticed them many years ago and spotted his stems, and now they all spot them, the spots getting bigger and bigger; and so it will be until some original genius arises who will not be content with other people's eyes, but will dare to look for himself, and he may perhaps, without abandoning Japanese methods, get nearer to nature, and start a renaissance in Japanese art.

He also remarks—

The lotus is one of the most difficult plants which it has ever been my lot to try to paint: the flowers are at their best only in the early morning, and each blossom, after it has opened, closes again before noon of the first day; on the second day its petals drop. The leaves are so large and so full of modelling that it is impossible to generalise them as a mass, each one has to be carefully studied, and every breath of wind disturbs their delicate balance and completely alters their forms. Besides this, their glaucous surface, like that of a cabbage leaf, reflects every passing phase of the sky, and is constantly changing in colour as clouds pass over.

Such is an artist's true appreciation.

No honour seems too great for this flower of Buddha, and we are told that you will be permitted, if you are fortunate enough to be among those who are admitted into Nirvana, or Paradise, to sit upon the lotus throne, leaving behind the dirt and dust of the world. In the days of old Japan, when the religious influence was stronger, and far more romantic than it is to-day, to sit together upon the lotus throne in Paradise was the customary dream of two lovers who wished to commit suicide.

Another honour for the lotus is that the Japanese dedicate their wonderful and awe-inspiring mountain Fuji-san to it, and call it Fugo Ho, meaning Lotus Peak. Thousands of their poets have sung praises of this lotus peak, but to our minds the words of Mrs. M'Neill Fenollosa will be easier to understand: "Now far beyond the grayness, to the west, the cone of Fuji flashes into splendour. It, too, is pink; its shape is the shape of a lotus bud, and the long fissures that plough the mountain-side are now but the delicate gold veining of a petal. Slowly it seems to open. It is the chalice of a new day, and the pledge of consecration." It would seem as though the opening of the lotus flower is the signal of the awakening of summer dawn and the opening of a new day.

In Chinese literature there is a legend of Teiko

LOTUS FLOWERS

who gathered his guests together on a midsummer day and put wine in the lotus leaves and let his guests drink it from the stems of the leaves. A truly romantic feast.

In Japan the leaves are used for dishes at the Soul's Festival in July; the dead spirits who return to this world from Hades are supposed to eat the offerings from the leaf dishes. The Japanese have a delicacy called *hasu meshi*—*hasu* meaning lotus, *meshi*, rice—consisting of the young and tender lotus leaves chopped fine and cooked with rice. They also eat the little fruit of the lotus, no larger than a pebble, which, contrary to most fruit, can be eaten raw when it is unripe, but gets so terribly hard as it ripens that it has to be cooked. The dried leaves seem to be valued as a drug, and also the vegetable-sellers wrap their vegetables in them. All this is too unromantic to be associated with the lotus, and I was better pleased to hear of the Japanese phrase *ben po*, meaning lotus step, which they associate with the light step of a beautiful woman. A pretty story of old China is told of the Lord Tokonko of the province Sei, who was extravagant in the extreme. He had as his mistress a lovely girl called Han hi. One day he made lotus petals of real gold and scattered them in his garden; then he called out to his mistress to let her step on them, and he was very happy to see his fair lady and his gold flowers equally well matched in beauty. Truly Han hi's "lotus step" must have been a wonder.

In saying farewell to the time of the lotus I feel I cannot do better than quote Mrs. Fenollosa's charming poem—

> For years, long years ago, on lake and river,
>   The lotus bloomed, with petals curl on curl
> Close folded; and to full perfection never
>   Had opened wide those lattices of pearl.
>
> Like fair white maids with finger-tips a-meeting,
>   Like wordless song unwed to music's art,
> They pierced the stream each morn in pallid greeting;
>   Then shrank in silence, for they had no heart.
>
> Above them, nightly, stars would lean, and hover
>   With gifts of whisper-rays, and kisses long;
> But all in vain, till one transcendent lover
>   Slid down from heaven among the startled throng.
>
> At morn the flowers stood still like pale nuns hushing:
>   But one among them throbbed her sweetness far,
> Like arms outspread the full-veined petals flushing,
>   For in her trembling heart there lay a star.
>
> And since that hour the sky rains lovers ever;
>   All day they rock within that soft embrace.
> At night the petals close; the stars up-quiver,
>   And sighing, seek their old accustomed place.

CHAPTER XV

THE CHRYSANTHEMUM

"SEE a *kiri* leaf fallen on the ground and know that autumn is with us" is a common saying in Japan. The leaves of the *kiri* (pawlonia) tree are so responsive to the spirit of autumn, which advances steadily till we see no garden flowers, no wild flowers, and have no longer the song of the insects, and one cannot fail to be impressed with some touch of sorrow; but the Japanese take sheer delight in the sadness of autumn, for soon the white frosts will be thick upon the ground and will turn the leaves of the maples on the mountain-side into a blaze of scarlet and gold, and then the *kiku* or chrysanthemum flowers will open.

The chrysanthemum has often been called the national flower of Japan, a rank more properly belonging to the cherry blossom; the mistake arises from the fact that the sixteen-petalled chrysanthemum is the Imperial emblem. The Japanese give a poetical reason for the choice of this especial flower as the Emperor's crest: as in olden days the chrysanthemum used to be called *Kukuri hana* or "Binding Flower," because as the blossoms tie or gather themselves together at the top, so the Mikado binds himself round the hearts and souls of his people; and it is a coincidence that the present Emperor's birthday falls in the *kiku* month (November). For a thousand years the chrysanthemum was admired as a retired beauty by the garden fence and under a simple mode of culture; but it became the flower of the rich to a great extent under the *Tokugawa* feudal régime, and of late years the culture of *kiku* or chrysanthemum is the greatest luxury. It would probably surprise one to know how much Count Okuma and Count Sakai, the two best known chrysanthemum raisers in Japan, spend annually upon their plants; and many other people have found the reason of their poverty in *kiku* culture. Though one cannot but admire any advance in horticulture, carried to such an extent it seems to me merely a degeneration, and this "retired nobleman of flowers" (the Japanese call their *kiku* one of the *sikunshi* or four

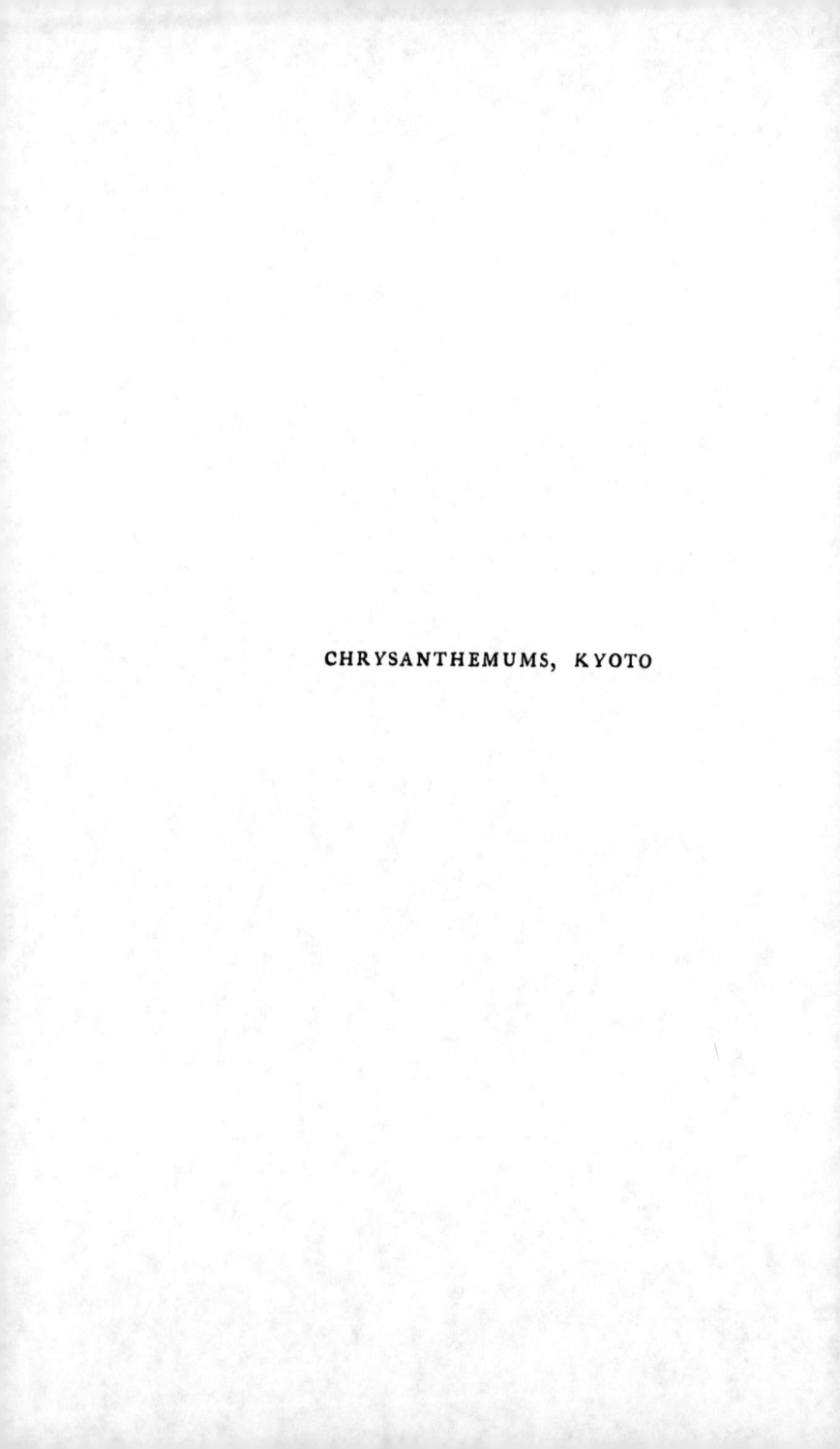

CHRYSANTHEMUMS, KYOTO

floral gentlemen, the other floral gentlemen being the plum, bamboo, and *ran* or orchid) will grow quite as well, and attain as great perfection, in some little humble dwelling which has only a miniature garden, provided the necessary time and care, not money, is given to the plants.

The chrysanthemum has always been much honoured by the Imperial Court, and even in the ninth century garden parties were held in the Palace gardens to do honour to the blossoms, even as in the present day a yearly chrysanthemum party is held in the Imperial grounds. In ancient days the guests sat drinking wine and composing odes to the blossoms, and the courtiers adorned their hair with *kiku* flowers, at these pastoral feasts. To-day these modern displays of chrysanthemum plants partake of our own conventional flower shows, the plants being arranged somewhat formally in long open rustic sheds; but the variety of colour, every imaginable shade being produced, and the profusion of form, also the immense size of some of the plants, one alone a few years ago bearing 1272 blooms, make a brilliant scene, different from any other flower show in the world; for where else would the plants have such a setting as in these beautiful Asakasa grounds, where the gorgeous colour of the maples rivals that of the chrysanthemums.

From an artistic point of view there is nothing to admire in the great chrysanthemum show which opens yearly at Dangozaka in Tokyo, and one cannot but agree with the poet Hoichi Shonin, who says—

> What an inferior heart of man!
> Lo! a waxwork chrysanthemum show!

However, one must admit the cleverness and some sort of art in these show pieces; and one cannot fail to be interested if only by watching the expectant faces of the thousands or tens of thousands of people who visit these different little shows. How the children's faces beam when they approach the place and see the thousands of flags and lanterns, gaily coloured curtains and stalls decorated with souvenirs in every conceivable form, of the day among the *kiku* flowers. The people are so enthusiastic over these puppet shows, which may be a scene from an old play, an act from history, or, most interesting of all, the newest occurrences of the day, all represented in chrysanthemums! In order to make the figures pot plants are used, not cut flowers, but splendid plants in full bloom, genuine plants, the roots of

THE CHRYSANTHEMUM

which are skilfully hidden or disguised. The colours of the flowers will be combined to represent the dresses, and indeed it is very interesting to see the figures being prepared in October when the plants are in bud, for each separate bud will be tied to the skeleton frame so that when the blossoms are open they form a compact mass of colour; and it is also very striking to notice the harmony of the colours, and then the bold lines made by a contrast of colour.

A year or two ago there was nothing more popular than war scenes of the Russian and Japanese campaign. One scene which has remained green in the memory of many a Japanese was the representation of the blocking of the harbour at Port Arthur, with Captain Hiroze, that valiant officer, and his fellow *keshitai* (determined to die) as the characters. It was composed of two thousand chrysanthemum roots; upon a sea of the royal flowers, dark coloured at the heart and rising to sprays of snow white, to form the crests of the waves and tossing billows, rode the boat manned by the heroes. The second scene was a tribute to the enemy: it represented the stalwart white-bearded Russian Admiral Makaroff, who, standing on the bridge, sword in hand, went down with his ship—a veritable storm of white flowers, dashed with red, and here and there a few sailors groping blindly. There was yet another show which represented the night after the great battle of Lia Yang, when the spirits of the dead soldiers appeared, all flower-clad, with white swords in their hands, with which to salute the sleeping fighters. Every year the showmen find some new subject in order to keep up the people's interest. Besides these dramatic shows, there are splendid specimen plants; and what I always admired about the large plants in Japan was the perfect foliage, the rather dwarfed growth, and the way in which all the blossoms on the plant open together. There is a plant called "Good Luck" bearing a thousand flowers, all from a single root, which is a great favourite, and certainly it is nothing short of a horticultural wonder. Their fancy names seemed very poetical, and I cannot refrain from quoting a few, with their translation, in the words of a Japanese—

"Look at the 'Princesses of the Blood' in a long stately row, tall and graceful, their proud flowers resplendent and white as the driven snow; or here is *Ake-no-sora*, 'the Sky at Dawn,' with a pale pink flower the colour of cherry blossoms; or *Asa hi no nami*, 'Waves in the Morning Sun,' because it has a pale reddish blossom; also *Yu hi kage*, 'Shadows of the Evening Sun,' with dull red blooms; and finally the pure white 'Companions of the Moon,' *Tsuki-no-tomo*." There appeared to be over 150 of these poetical flowers.

But do not imagine that it is only in the gardens of the rich or arranged as waxwork puppet shows that you will find chrysanthemums, for surely, if that were the case, little pleasure would be derived from their beloved *kiku*. It has been said of the Japanese, "It is not the plant he loves, but the effect that the plant enables him to attain." This may be true of plants in relation to the landscape garden, where everything must be according to the rubric or laws of gardening, but surely it is not true of chrysanthemum plants. Many an enthusiast have I known to whom his *kiku* was his most valued and cherished possession, and daily were the "Plants of the Four Seasons" (a fancy name for chrysanthemums on account of their period of growth extending through all the seasons) tended with loving hands. We are told of a great man in the days of the Min dynasty who, tired of struggling with the world and life, gave up his rank and retired to some forgotten spot, entirely in order to enjoy the sight of the chrysanthemum in his garden and a jug of wine; and the greatest delight of his life was to see the flowers bedewed in the morning light, and to exchange his poet's faith and love with this "nobleman of flowers." Perhaps in these days when the curse of modern civilisation is spreading throughout the land we shall not see many such enthusiasts as Yen Mei; but there are still many chrysanthemum lovers, many to whom the first week in November is the best week of the year. Just as the Japanese admire the flower for its noble bearing, so did I admire the bearing of their owners; however humble the dwelling, however small the collection, the proud possessor seemed always to be one of "Nature's noblemen"; never did I encounter such warm and true hospitality combined with dignity and grace as during the *kiku* month from my chrysanthemum hosts. One scene especially seems to have remained graven into my memory, in that land of surprises.

A friend offered to take me to see some especially fine chrysanthemums; their owner, he said, was celebrated for their culture; and he led me through the whole length and breadth of the fish market, I imagined only in order to make a short cut to our destination, but no! we stopped in front of a large fish-stall, and at the magic word *kiku*

A CHRYSANTHEMUM GARDEN

the owner's face beamed with delight, for surely here was a fellow-enthusiast, even though she is a "foreigner," come to admire his beloved flowers. He signed to me to thread my way past the somewhat unappetising-looking fish, and, as though at the touch of a fairy wand, the scene changed. A paper shutter slid back and the beauty revealed beyond surpassed anything that mortal could imagine—little corners and flashes of loveliness in all directions. At the very entrance were grouped a few splendid plants, each bloom perfection itself, and then with cries of "Irasshai irasshai" (Welcome, welcome) and the regulation greeting of "Please come in, my house is yours" from every side, I entered, crossing the cool matting, past a tiny court filled with the treasured plants and adorned with a hanging iron lantern which filled my soul with envy, through the spotless rooms with the alcove and the regulation *kakemono* and the *tokonoma* on which stood a flower arrangement of *Baka sakura* ("Fool Cherry," because it has come into flower at the wrong season), to the court beyond, where stood the famous collection. The whole scene diffused a feeling of perfect contentment as I sat upon the regulation *fukusa* in the place of honour, the place corresponding to the

"Stone of Contemplation" of every Japanese garden, the one spot from which the whole effect is seen to best advantage. The plants were grouped in front of the family shrine, and to protect them from the autumn storms a light roofing of paper and bamboo had been erected; the little garden contained a few stepping-stones, a bronze water basin, a few lanterns, and to screen off any possible view of anything suggestive of fish was a delicate bamboo screen-fence. The blossoms seemed to represent every colour, shape, and size that it was possible for a chrysanthemum to assume, all perfectly grown plants. Some varieties were quite new to me—tall, slender-growing stems crowned with little fluffy blossoms not suggesting the usual form of a chrysanthemum; another, which when fully developed would form a complete pyramid of closely packed petals of a dark crimson hue, was awarded the place of honour, as there were only two other plants of the same kind in all Japan. I noticed some plants bearing a label which differed from any others, and then I was told that each year a special messenger is sent by the Emperor to choose a few plants from this humble fishmonger's garden to be added to the Imperial collection. The labelled plants formed this year's offering to his Mikado, and small wonder they were the pride of the house; and I too was impressed by the feeling that in the floral kingdom, as in a Higher Kingdom, all men are equal, as the *kiku* flowers had grown as well, if not better, in this lowly dwelling as in the Emperor's vast domains.

I cannot recall any incident during all my stay in Japan which gave me more pleasure than my visit to this humble home, and as I left, laden with little *kiku* cakes and with the prescribed compliments, obeisances, and sincere admiring exclamations over the flowers, I had every intention of availing myself of the repeated invitations to "Please come again." The plants one day were in their full glory, the great heads of perfect blossom had only just attained perfection, when I was told that this was to be their last day of life, on the morrow every plant would be cut down. I exclaimed in horror at this apparent slaughter of the innocents in their prime of life, but it was explained to me that the sacrifice was necessary in order to secure the cuttings for the next year's plants. I could not help thinking that if I had nursed the cherished plants all through the year, shading them from the intense heat of summer on the house-top, never allowing them to know the want of water, I could not have spared the blossoms in their prime even for the sake of the next year's growth.

Many another peaceful little garden I can recall where I was welcomed with all the grace and hospitality suggestive of Old Japan, and to this day apparently inseparable from the lovers of chrysanthemums. Two neighbours vied with each other in *kiku* culture, their houses only separated by a few yards. In one, an old man, whose bearing and manners suggested the Daimyo of olden days, sat as if he too, tired of the world, had retired with the sole companionship of his plants. Very lovely was his tiny garden, with the plants just grouped in front of the two rooms which constituted his entire house, and there he sat in quiet contemplation, or bowing low to meet some new-comer who had come to admire his flowers, and all seemed welcome, strangers and friends alike, as long as they loved the blossoms. Here might be seen the great sun-like *Nihon Ichi* ("First in Japan"), white and yellow; and there is *Haruna Kasumi*, like its name, suggesting spring haze, or *Natsu gumo* ("Summer Clouds"); but with all this infinite variety I noticed that, like in China, where by "the yellow flower" is meant the chrysanthemum of that country, so here in Japan, the yellow blossoms

CHRYSANTHEMUMS

THE CHRYSANTHEMUM

seemed the most prized, though the pure white is a close rival for popularity, their blooms thick with the morning dew reminding us of the fairy who lived only by sipping the dews upon the *kiku* flowers. How beautiful, too, are these white blossoms in death when the frost has made their petals turn slowly to a crimson colour.

Across the road I found another little sanctuary, another home for the flowers. Here a tiny tea-room was the point of vantage, and from there I gazed, sipping tea from the daintiest of tiny cups. What an ideal place to sit and meditate and wonder over the goodness of things! Below was the rocky bed of a stream, but it was a dry river-bed, only white pebbles represented the stream, and on the banks were grouped the plants, forming a sheet of colour—great gorgeous blossoms, not of such mammoth and unnatural proportions as our show blooms, but every kind were here, single, loose, or double; stiff, flopping, or erect; borne in a veritable harvest.

Yet another humble dwelling I remember where the plants were grouped with consummate art. In every garden there should be a keynote in the scheme, and here the keynote was the view of Hieisan: framed between the blossoms, which grew in a great foaming mass, rose the great mountain, as though it were the guardian of the garden. The plants had brilliantly rewarded a loyal devotion, and as I turned away I realised the manner in which Japanese love their flowers.

As I sat admiring their gardens, my friends told me many fairy stories and legends connected with the *kiku*. Perhaps one of the prettiest is called "The Chrysanthemum Promise." Samon Hase, a scholar and samurai, offered a night's lodging to a gentleman from the western country, and his guest suddenly fell ill. Samon promised the sick man to give him every help: "Be easy in your thought. Above all, be not discouraged!" The sick man was Soemon Akana, who had been with a friend on a mission which failed, and his friend was killed, and he was on his way home when he fell ill. Samon and Soemon quickly became friends, and finally they promised to be as brothers to each other. The latter stayed until he grew well; and then he said he must go back to his native province of Izume, but promised that he would return again and stay with Samon for the rest of his days. He said firmly that the day of the chrysanthemum feast (ninth of September in the old calendar) would be the day of his return.

THE CHRYSANTHEMUM

September came, and on the ninth Samon rose early to make preparations for his returning brother. The sun began slowly to set, but Soemon did not come. Samon thought he would retire to bed, but as he looked out once more into the night he noticed that the moon was hiding behind the hill, and he saw a curious black shadow coming towards him with the wind. It was Soemon Akana.

Samon made his brother sit by the chrysanthemum vase in the place of honour, and Akana said, "I have no word to express my thanks for your kindness. But pray listen, and do not doubt me: I am not a living person but only a shadow"; and he told how he had been put in prison, but finding no other means of escape he killed himself. "As I was told," he said, "that a spirit could travel a thousand miles a day, so I killed myself, and rode on the wind to see you on this day of my chrysanthemum promise." I felt if this legend were taught in the schools of to-day a moral might be pointed with advantage on the subject of keeping appointments and promises, which is not a strong point with the modern Japanese.

There is another pretty story of two brothers who had always lived together in the north of Japan. The time came for them to separate, and when the younger one was about to start on his journey south, they wept bitterly, and said that each would keep the half of a chrysanthemum plant in memory of the other, and thereby recall the happy days they had spent together. The brothers afterwards planted the halves in two gardens, one in the north, the other in the south; but the blossoms, it is said, kept the original shape of the half of a chrysanthemum for ever.

The chrysanthemum is so associated with the story of O Kiku, the little maid of Himeji, in the province of Banshu, that I feel I cannot do better than tell it in the words of Lafcadio Hearn —

Himeji contains the ruins of a great castle of thirty turrets; and a daimyo used to dwell therein, whose revenue was one hundred and fifty-six thousand koku of rice. Now, in the house of one of that daimyo's chief retainers was a maid-servant of good family, whose name was O Kiku; and the Kiku signifies a chrysanthemum flower. Many precious things were entrusted to her charge, and among other things ten costly dishes of gold. One of these was suddenly missed and could not be found; and the girl, being responsible therefor, and knowing not otherwise how to prove her innocence, drowned herself in a well. But ever thereafter her ghost, returning nightly, could be heard counting the dishes slowly, with sobs: *Ichi-mai, Ni-mai, San-mai, Yo-mai, Go-mai, Roku-mai, Shichi-mai, Hachi-mai, Ku-mai.*

Then there would be heard a despairing cry and a loud burst of weeping, and again the girl's voice counting the dishes plaintively: "One, two, three, four, five, six, seven, eight, nine."

Her spirit passed into the body of a strange little insect, whose head faintly resembled that of a ghost with long dishevelled hair; and it is called *O kiku-mushi*, or the "fly of O Kiku"; and it is found, they say, nowhere save in Himeji. A famous play was written about O Kiku, which is still acted in all the popular theatres, entitled *Banshu-O-Kiku-no-Sara-Ya-shiki*, or "The Manor of the Dish of O Kiku of Banshu."

But there are people who say that Banshu is Bancho, an ancient quarter of Tokyo (Yedo). The people of Himeji claim, however, that part of their city now called Go-Ken-Yashiki is the site of the ancient manor of the story. And it is deemed unlucky to cultivate chrysanthemums in Go-Ken-Yashiki.

CHAPTER XVI

THE MAPLE LEAVES

THE Japanese quite rightly give the name of *Ko haru* or Little Spring to the Indian summer, Keats's season of mists and mellow fruitfulness; for indeed those beautiful weeks in November are incomparable, the heavy damp heat of the summer has lifted, the sky is clear and blue, the atmosphere is light, and the freshness of spring seems to have returned to revive the dying year. They say, "Here is the right end, since we had a right start." These fortunate people who rejoice in the beauty of spring beginning with the plum blossoms born out of the frost, now have the autumn with the *momiji* or maple leaves to complete the floral season, and the red leaves will be the beauty of the maturing year. Autumn weaves her red and gold brocade and spreads it on mountain and tree, the whole country being alight with the scarlet

THE SCARLET MAPLE

THE MAPLE LEAVES

and gold of the *momiji*; for not only the maples are called *momiji*, but any tree whose leaves turn red in their last moment of life.

Throughout the land there are favourite places where the holiday-maker holds his maple-viewing feast. The trees at Nikko are probably the first to turn, and by the middle of October this little mountain village will be visited by a throng of sight-seers, all bent on viewing the red leaves; and here truly not only the maples, but every tree seems to wear its mantle of autumn brocade, making a splendid contrast to the bronze green of the cryptomerias. The first touch of frost will have made the trees blush, so the Japanese say—it being a favourite expression of theirs, when a blush of modesty spreads over a girl's cheeks, to say that "she scatters red leaves on her face,"—and then will come the first light fall of snow or a rude wind storm and scatter all the silent beauty of the valley. If you would continue your maple feast, you must go farther south, say to Oji near Tokyo, where you will find a whole glen filled with nothing but maples. No other *momiji* will dispute their fiery splendour; and there, in a little rustic tea-shed, you can sit and gaze at the gorgeous scene below, and wonder whether it is more beautiful to see the leaves like lace-work against the sky, or to look down on the great spreading branches shading the stream below. Here and there will be a tree that does not deserve the name of *momiji*, for it has no red leaves. Possibly it is a descendant of the celebrated maple-tree of the Shomeiji temple at Mutsuura, which turned a glorious colour when summer had scarcely waned, in order to earn the praise of the poet Chunagon Tamesuke, who went to seek the beauties of the early maple. The tree being fully satisfied with the admiration of the poet, remained green for ever after; for did not the poet say—

> How did this one tree thus get coloured?
> This one garden maple-tree
> Showing Autumn before the mountain trees!"

It is always said that the poetical spirit of Tamesuke moved the responsive heart of the maple-tree.

Kyoto, the old capital, with its history of centuries, is celebrated for the numerous places renowned for maple-viewing. All through the early part of November there is feasting, combined possibly with mushroom-gathering, a favourite pastime connected with the viewing of the *momiji*. Near by there is Tsuten Bridge, where the sound

THE MAPLE LEAVES

of revelry will greet you as you approach, and there will be the inevitable little tea-stalls, decorated with curtains printed with a few flaunting maple leaves, lanterns ornamented with the same red leaves, and branches of the trees adorned with red and yellow paper leaves; bearing a streamer with the name of the place, or possibly a diminutive paper lantern, to carry away as a souvenir of the day's feasting. If you want a wider field and more extensive view, remember Takao is waiting in all its glory to greet you; there a great stream of colour winds away down the valley following the course of the little mountain torrent. You must rise early for maple-viewing, to see the trees while the sun is on them; when the sun goes it seems as though he takes half the beauty of the *momiji* away with him, only to return it on the morrow, it is true, if the clear bright days will last through the short season of the *momiji*. Any night a cruel frost may come, and next day the ground will be covered with a scarlet carpet, reminding one of the story of that great lover of maple leaves, the Emperor Takakura-no-In. He planted the maple-trees at Kita-no-Jin, and called the spot Momiji Yama or Maple-leaf Hill. His great delight was to see the red leaves which carpet the ground with autumn glory. One morning his unpoetical gardeners swept away the fallen leaves, and the officers of the Imperial household were awestruck, as they were sure the Emperor would visit the hill to see the red leaves which might have been cast down by the night wind. He went to the hill, and the officers appealed to him to have pity on the gardeners' ignorance. "It reminds me," said the Emperor, "of the famous verse by Ri Tai Haku which runs—

> We will warm the wine under the maple-trees;
> We will burn up the maple leaves."

Such is the song of autumn: "how lovely the gardeners' hearts in gathering the leaves to warm their hearts and wine." So not only was the stupidity of the gardeners excused, but happily their action was approved. Had the gardeners such poetical hearts? I doubt it; rather, how forgiving was the heart of the Emperor.

Arashi Yama must not be omitted from the maple-viewing feast. Here the beauties of Nature summon us twice a year—in spring to visit the cherry blossoms, in autumn to view the *momiji*. At the latter season the trees are dressed in red, and the water will be red too, so thickly is it carpeted with the fallen leaves. If one takes a

VIEWING THE MAPLES

THE MAPLE LEAVES

boat to cross the water one feels ashamed to see the rent it makes in the "autumn brocade," for the boat will cut a track right through the thin carpet of leaves, of which the poet says—

> The hurdle that the wind has built
> Over the mountain river,
> Is nothing but the maple leaves
> Not run down the stream.

At Mino there are nothing but maples as far as the eye can reach, on and on down the glen, an incredible blaze of colour. But it was not in these great masses, though no one can deny their gorgeous splendour, that the maple gave me most pleasure; it was rather in some quiet garden away from the sound of feasting that a few trees of the choicer and therefore even more brilliant coloured varieties afforded me most enjoyment. I am thinking now of a warm November day when I had been bidden to take part in a tea ceremony, with all its quaint ceremonial and code of rules. Sitting in the little simple open tea-room—for does not the law forbid any elaborate decoration in the room set apart for tea ceremonies, and must not the room always be open on one, if not two sides? —while trying to conform to the rigid etiquette of this pretty ceremony of drinking tea in a preternaturally slow manner, when it was no longer my turn to admire in regulation words one of the articles used in the tea-making, my eye wandered to the scene outside, where, hanging over a miniature cascade, adding effect to the tiny rushing torrent, stood the maple-trees, surely the brightest I had ever seen. Maple-trees are most necessary for the Japanese landscape garden, especially when, as is usually the case, the style of the garden is to reproduce natural scenery. The Japanese have a saying that autumn comes from the west, therefore the maple-tree, the true representative of autumn, should be planted on a hill towards the west, so that it will welcome autumn promptly, and also in order that the reddening leaves may receive additional splendour from the setting sun. Here, in the glow of the western sun, it seemed incredible that the little trees were only clad in leaves, not in flowers, for their colour was as bright as, if not brighter than, the brilliant azaleas which had been the pride of the garden in the flower month of May.

The nursery gardens are gay with splendid specimens of the much-prized dwarf maple-trees, and every lover of these little trees will have a few plants of *momiji* in his collection. Some there may be which had, as it were, been born with scarlet leaves—in spring the leaves having opened a fiery red, their colour waning as the year wanes; others which had only green leaves in the spring will, like true *momiji*, have got more and more fiery in colour until the shadow of death comes over them. Innumerable varieties there appeared to be, distinguished by the shape of their leaves and the tone of their colour.

The changing life of the maple, Miss Scidmore tells us, has been made use of by "the Japanese coquette, who sends her lover a leaf or branch of maple to signify that, like it, her love has changed." If you call a Japanese baby and it opens its tiny hand, they call it "a hand of maple leaf."

Throughout November the whole land is redolent of *momiji*; not only will the red leaves on the trees greet you at every turn, but you will be offered tea out of little cups painted with just one red leaf, the cakes represent maple leaves, the Geishas will all have soft crêpe kimonos decked with a pattern of the flaunting leaves, or their stiff silk obis will represent Nature's "autumn brocade." In the theatres the romantic play called *Momiji gari*, or Maple-leaf Viewing, is played, the stage being gorgeously decorated with maple-trees. Possibly because it is the last flower-viewing feast of the year, the *momiji*-viewing is almost the most popular, and when the last leaf falls the feasters will have to rest until the plum blossoms are opening, as Nature even in this land of flowers must take her winter's rest.

CHAPTER XVII

THE BAMBOO

WHAT would the Japanese do without the bamboo? Indeed so extensive is the part played by the bamboo, not only in the beautifying of the land, but in her domestic economy, that the question is rather, what does it *not* do? The number of species of bamboo in Japan at present is stated to be fifty, not including numerous other varieties and sports; among them thirty-nine are indigenous, and the others have been imported at various times from Korea, China, or the Lu-chu Islands. From time immemorial the Japanese have not regarded the bamboo as a tree—it forms a category apart, and they speak of "trees and bamboos"; they say it belongs to the grasses, and is just a giant grass and nothing more. It is indeed a beautiful and wonderful grass with a rate of growth which cannot be compared to that of any other member of the vegetable kingdom; some species are said to show a growth of several feet in the course of four-and-twenty hours, reminding one of one of the many ghastly forms of Chinese tortures, when a man is pegged to the ground on the top of a sprouting bamboo, whose shoots are so strong that they will grow right through the man's body in the course of a single night.

Most people persist in regarding the bamboo as a tender tropical plant unable to stand our bitter Northern winters; but there must be many hardy species, as often they may be seen bending under the weight of snow, even in the northern provinces of Japan, where the snow-fall is measured not in inches but in feet. Many varieties there are which no doubt would not flourish, varieties associated in one's mind with the gardens of Trinidad or the well-known Perediniya gardens in Ceylon, but these tropical species should not be confounded with the hardy forms which find their home in Japan and China. In the *Bamboo Garden*, the author has viewed the bamboo chiefly from the standpoint of acclimatisation in England, especially in the damper western and southern counties, for dampness seems essential to the life of a bamboo; in fact, so greedy is it of moisture that in many

THE BAMBOO

countries where the rainfall in summer is small the bamboo is condemned, as it sucks the life from surrounding plants. One of the commonest and most beautiful species, the *moso dake* or feathery bamboo, was an import from China; it is so named from its golden stem and overhanging plume-like fronds appearing like a group of feathers; and it is used to a great extent as one of the features of a Japanese garden. Other imported species are the *hochiku* tree or square bamboo, and the *samo chiku*, whose stems when young are of a bright red hue. These bamboos were imported for industrial uses or for the adornment of rich men's gardens; and besides these there is a long list of other native and foreign varieties.

To the bamboo the Japanese owe much, for it would seem to be the cause of much of their clever constructive work; properly handled it will do most things, but it is necessary to understand its proper treatment and peculiar qualities. How puzzled an English carpenter would be if he were asked to construct one of those delicate, dainty little tea-rooms entirely of bamboo! which it is possible to do.

The larger species will provide a combination of lightness and strength, which makes them an admirable framework for houses, and an intermediate size will make ornamental doors or panelling, the varying height of the joints forming a natural pattern; while the ornamental floor of the verandah can be made of bamboo. The water-pipes will be of bamboo, as they neither rust like iron nor get hot like wood; and the carpenter will tell you that bamboo nails serve better for certain purposes than metal ones, being non-conductors of heat and non-corrosible. The thick poles seem remarkably strong, and are always used for carrying heavy weights and for punt poles. The national flag of the Rising Sun is sure to be flying from a bamboo. A complete list of its uses would appear to be never-ending, but it is amusing to think how many things in daily use in Japan are made of this "grass." The smaller kinds make fans and baskets, penholders and tobacco-pipe stems, umbrellas and coolies' hats, ladles and delicate whisks for stirring the "honourable tea" at a tea ceremony, chopsticks for everyday use, and bird-cages, fishing-rods and walking-sticks, flutes and trumpets, every description of toy, and ornaments of innumerable kinds. Sandals and the soles of clogs are made from the dried sheath of the culm of the young bamboo, and it also serves for wrapping up such things as rice sandwiches,

THE BAMBOO

meat and cake, or anything which is liable to stain its receptacle. Fish-baskets made of split bamboo have a clean, cool lining of *sasa* or bamboo grass, a variety which grows on hills or by the wayside; in spring its leaves are of the brightest green, but become edged with white as the year wanes, producing the effect of a variegated form. Other kinds, split and twisted, make strong hawsers, and are even used in rural districts in the construction of bridges; and yet another kind is boiled and flattened out into trays which are much prized. The young shoots are boiled and eaten, and taste rather like flavourless asparagus. So there is no end to the uses of the bamboo. As mentioned elsewhere, it is one of the "four gentlemen of the floral kingdom," being associated with the pine, orchid, and plum. Its never-fading colour causes it to be compared to the virtue of man or the chastity of woman. O Take, meaning honourable bamboo, is one of the popular names for a Japanese girl; and their writers and poets use it frequently as a *nom de plume*.

One of the first stories of Japanese literature, in the tenth century, was called *Taketori Monogatari*. Taketori, meaning bamboo gatherer, is the story of an old man who made his living by making bamboo ware. One day he saw in the woods a bamboo with a shining stem; he split it open, and discovered in one of the joints a beautiful little maiden only three inches in height. He took this wonderful little bamboo maiden home and adopted her as his daughter, giving her the name of Kagujakime or the "Shining Lady." She grew up to womanhood, and her marvellous beauty attracted many admirers. She assigned a quest to each of them, under the promise that she would marry the suitor who should succeed in accomplishing the task allotted to him. One lover was told to fetch Buddha's begging bowl of stone from India; another, to bring her a branch of the tree with roots of silver, stem of gold, and fruit of jewels, which grew in the fabulous island paradise of Mount Horai; from the third she required a garment made of the fur of the fire-rat, supposed to be non-inflammable; a fourth was to get the shining jewel of many hues from the dragon's head; and the fifth a swallow's cowry shell. It is no wonder that they all failed. This bamboo maiden was then wooed by the Emperor, but equally in vain, though they remained on friendly terms and kept up an exchange of sentimental *uta* poems. She was eventually taken up to heaven in a flying chariot, brought

THE BAMBOO

by her relations in the moon; for it seems she had been banished to earth for an offence which she had committed. Thus this wonderful "Shining Lady," from the joint of a bamboo, only three inches high —disappears.

Another bamboo fairy-story dear to the hearts of all Japanese children is that of the Tongue-cut Sparrow. Sparrows and bamboos have been the closest friends from an unknown age, and we hear the song "The sparrows sing on the bamboos so sweetly." The bamboo and sparrows combined form the crest of the great lord of Sendai. Any Japanese child will tell you how the poor little sparrow was driven out of his bamboo cage after losing his little tongue, because he had eaten starch for washing clothes belonging to a mean old woman. When her husband returned home from the mountain and learned the fate of his pet bird, he said, "He meant nothing bad in eating your starch. When you could so easily have forgiven him, how could you be so cruel as to cut off his tongue and drive him away? If I had been here he should never have been punished so severely: this heartless deed was done because I was away. Alas! how can I help shedding tears?" He started out the next morning to find his lost pet, singing—

> "Tongue-cut sparrow,
> Where are you?
> Where is your lodging,
> Where are you?
> Tongue-cut sparrow,
> Chu, Chu, Chu."

The sparrow soon recognised the voice of his master, and jumped out of his house, exclaiming, "Pray enter my humble home!" The house was made, of course, of bamboo bush, as sparrows' houses always are, and the pillars and roofs were also of bamboo. The sparrow said, "You have come a long way to see me. How can I thank you enough! I cannot help shedding tears of joy." The story goes on to tell of all the strange things the sparrow did, which turned to fortune for the old man. However, when his wife came singing the same song, her greediness made her bring a heavy basket instead of a light one, as her husband had done. So when she opened the cover she found not gold and treasures as her husband had done, but a monster with three eyes, a giant toad, a viper, and other terrible reptiles.

Another simple Chinese story is from the so-called "Four-and-Twenty Paragons of Filial Piety." There was a man whose filial piety was so wonderful that his true heart moved even Heaven

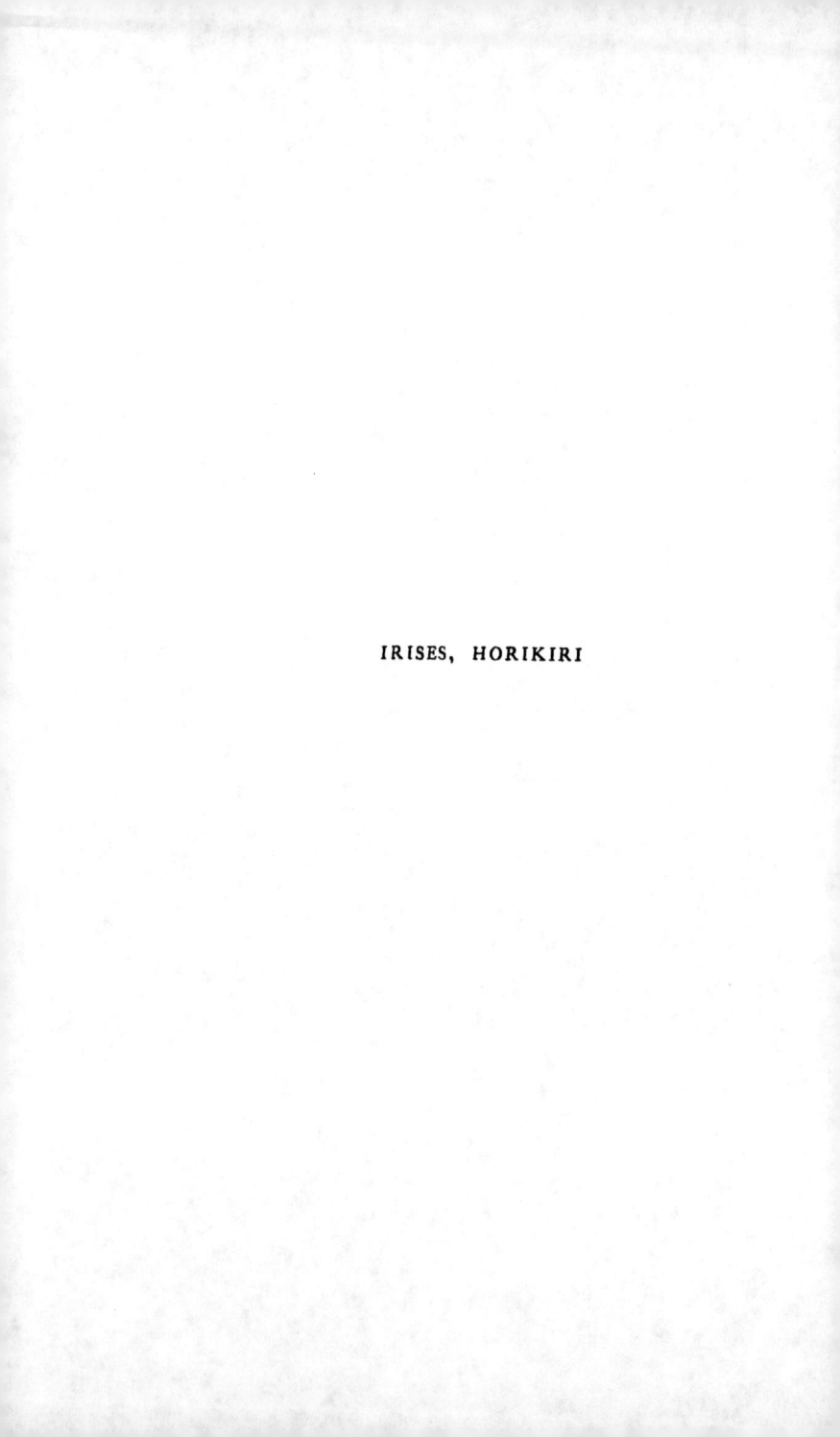

IRISES, HORIKIRI

and Earth. His old mother wished to eat the tender bamboo shoots one cold winter day when it was absurd to try and get them. This man started towards a bush of bamboo to look into it, and there, to his great surprise, he found plenty of the new shoots. It is said that his great filial piety moved the hearts of the bamboo bushes and they answered his true devotion voluntarily. Filial piety is the virtue *par excellence* of the Eastern world; such a story is very popular with the Japanese people, and is read to their children to encourage their devotion towards their old parents.

Like its associate the pine, the bamboo plays an important part in the art of flower arrangement, though there again we are told by Mr. Conder that strictly speaking it is regarded as neither a tree nor a plant. Possibly the most important of all its uses in the art lies in the fact that so many of the vessels made for holding the flowers are made of bamboo, some merely plain sections, others of the most fanciful description. Some of the baskets of Chinese origin were made of split bamboo, and were so much prized in Japan that high prices were given for antique specimens. So complicated an art does this one of floral arrangement appear to be, that it would require many years to learn the correct choice of the vessels into which certain flowers should be arranged, which flowers are suitable as offerings for ceremonial occasions, the correct combination of flowers and trees or shrubs, and the shape in which they are to be arranged. The list of bamboo vessels alone, with their fanciful names, would require months to master, and no doubt in each separate one only certain flowers are permissible. The original use of bamboo flower-vases seems to date from the days of Yoshimasa, and, like so many other things, started by being merely simple sections of a thick bamboo cut so that the bottom was closed by a natural division, and the cylinders were a foot or so high. Then came the invention of innumerable fancy forms: portions of the sides were notched out, side apertures were introduced, and sometimes four or five compositions were arranged in one vase. The names chiefly refer to some fancied resemblance in the general shape—so we read of the Lion's Mouth shape, the Travelling-Pillow shape, Chinese Gateway, Shark's Mouth, Wild Geese's Gateway, Lantern shape, Five Storey shape, Crane's Neck shape, and Monkey shape; in fact a list of many pages in length might be given of all the varieties, but from the above will be seen the extreme fancifulness of the supposed resemblance. Then, again, do not imagine that the much-prized baskets are just a basket and nothing more. They also assume fanciful names and shapes, such as the Raincoat basket, so called because the frayed top hanging over the edge is suggestive of the collar of a Japanese farmer's straw raincoat; Cicada and Butterfly baskets, from their resemblance to the insect; and the Hood-shaped basket, suggesting the shape of the hoods worn by Japanese women in cold weather.

Then we come to perhaps the prettiest of all, the boat-shaped vessels, which are suspended by a cord or chain. The simplest of these are bamboo tubes splayed off at the ends, hollowed out, and hung horizontally. These, one would have thought, were probably their original form as conceived by Yoshimasa whilst observing children sailing toy boats filled with flowers; but the more elaborate bronze vases in exact imitation of ships and junks came first, and the simpler ones are of later origin. Some attribute the first use of boat vases to the fact that the celebrated philosopher Soami, to please his patron Yoshimasa, took a bronze vessel of accidental resemblance to a boat, and by his arrangement of the flowers suggested the idea of a sailing vessel. The regent was so pleased with this novel flower arrangement that Soami devoted his attention to drawing up certain rules with regard to boat arrangements.

Bamboo rafts formed of bamboos of different lengths tied together to hang horizontally, either supporting a basket of flowers, or with one of the tubes hollowed so as to hold the stems of the branches, show yet another way in which the bamboo is used. Such a raft laden with cherry blossoms is arranged to suggest the mountain scenery of Arashiyama and the flower-laden craft in the season of cherry blossoms. The correct use of the branches of bamboo as a decoration would appear to be no less complicated than the choice of the vessels. A portion of the round stem or tube is selected and only a few leaf-clad twigs are permitted to remain, and, according to the occasion for which the arrangement is being made, the tube must be splayed or cut horizontally. For instance, for wedding feasts the cut must be concealed by leaves, as the sight of it would be considered unlucky and suggestive of severed friendship. Regulations also exist as to the number of twigs or leaves which are to be left on the stems,—three or five as a rule; and yet further rules as to the number of leaves to be left on these same twigs. Three combinations are approved, known as the Fish tail, Goldfish tail, and Flying Geese shape, which consists of three sloping leaves suggestive of the outline of a wild goose in flight. Probably the best known combination is that of the pine, bamboo, and plum, as it is specially employed at the New Year, when almost every house in Japan will have such a combination arranged on the *tokonoma*. Enough has been said to show the bewildering number of laws and regulations that surround this especial art, and it is not to be wondered at that Mr. Conder is probably the only foreigner who has ever mastered the subject, as indeed it requires years of study before a flower arrangement completed by the hand of one who is not a Japanese could hope to pass muster before the critical eye of the professor.

CHAPTER XVIII

THE PINE-TREE

THE pine-trees—*Matsu-no-ki*—of Japan are so closely and inseparably associated with the country, in the beauty of the landscape, the national customs and the national art, that it seems impossible when describing the floral year to omit the pine-trees, surely the grandest and noblest decoration of the land. They seem to welcome you to Japan, for as your ship glides up the Inland Sea the pine-trees will greet you on every side, the mountains will be clad with their eternal green, every island will have some venerable trees twisted and bent by storms and age. To the Japanese the pine is the king of trees, full of poetical suggestion and perfectly incomparable; and certainly it would be impossible to imagine Japan without her pine-trees. The impressive grandeur of every Shinto temple, every Buddhist shrine, is deepened by the grey-green trees standing in their silent gardens; they seem a necessity to such august places. Think of the pines at Uyeno or at Shiba; their merit is as great as the cherry-trees in the parks; to them and the cryptomeria belongs the task of guarding all the temples of the land. Every Tokugawa feudal castle had a moat bordered with pine-trees—how many have now been swept away and nothing left but a meaningless waste! The Imperial palace is chiefly shaded by the trees, their heavy foliage suggesting the depth of the forest. To-day every common house and garden has its guardian pine-tree at the gate.

The Japanese are very fond of visiting special *meisho* or "famous places," and how many of these places have been made famous by the beauty of their pine-trees, for where is the spot of natural beauty in all the country which has no pines? The three most "famous places" owe their beauty to water and the pines, nothing else. The great *hokku* poet Basho found himself quite unable to sing his "seventeen syllables" at Matsushima, the land of the pine-clad islands; he was a wandering poet who left a line or two wherever he went, but here he considered his silence was the greatest song of praise for the place, which he said was the best in Japan. He wrote in his diary: "One isle stands pointing up to the sky; another bows crawling over the waves; one parts at the left, another joins again at the right. The green beauty of the pine-trees is superb; the branches and leaves are bent quite naturally by the wind and tide." Indeed I do not wonder that he found himself unable to describe this land of fairy isles within the limits of seventeen syllables, for given unlimited space and an unlimited number of syllables it is hard to convey any idea of the beauty of the scene. Eight and its compounds are favourite round numbers with the Japanese, so they assured me that there were 808 in all of these tiny islands; and surely no one would dispute it. Each great winter storm sweeping in from the Pacific makes one or more of these toy islands crumble and disappear; but the sea makes rapid inroads and hollows out fresh archways or fresh tunnels, so very quickly a promontory breaks off and forms a new island, to be given a new fancy name, thus keeping up the traditional number. In every available nook stands one of the storm-bent trees which have given name and fame to the locality, whose praises have been sung by

PINE-TREE AT MATSUSHIMA

thousands of poets and how many *kakemono*; screens and *fusuma* have been adorned with the conventional views of Matsu-shima; Oshima, decorated with its shrines and lanterns, and connected with the mainland by a slender bridge, half hidden by the leaning trees, is perhaps the most favourite theme for the artist and poet. The pines of Matsu-shima appeared to be all the variety known as *Pinus densiflora*—possibly the most beautiful of all, with its red stems and deep-green foliage.

I read of them described as in the "form of crouching dragons, red-scaled and rough, with fins of living green." Another of the three "famous places" of the Empire is associated purely with pine and water; for to the eye of the unpoetical foreigner Ama-no-Hashi-date, a spot where thousands of Japanese congregate annually, is nothing but a long narrow sandy peninsula with an avenue of leaning pine-trees on either side. Its poetical name, meaning the Bridge or Ladder of Heaven, was given to the spot in allusion to *Ama-no-uki-hashi* or Floating Bridge of Heaven, whereon Izanagi and Iganami stood when they stirred up the brine of the primeval chaos with their jewelled spear, the drops from which consolidated into the first island of the Japanese archipelago. Though the name of the locality is not derived from its association with the pine, there are many points from whence the prospect is most admired, such as Ippon Matsu (One Pine-tree) which have been called after the trees; and under the branches of this solitary tree the poet may sit and meditate and compose his ode to the lovely scene. The long narrow spit, the tranquil water, and a few moored junks is another favourite scene for the Japanese artist.

To the European the last of the three great sights will appeal more surely, for no one could fail to be lost in admiration of Miyajima or Itsukushima, the holy island of the Inland Sea. It well deserves its rank among the famous places. The Japanese are said to admire it most under snow. I have never seen it under those conditions; but I can imagine no more beautiful scene than meets the eye in the early morning of a scorching August day, when the sampan floats across to this pine-clad island, the light haze just clearing from the woods, the great temple looking as if it were floating on the water, and the noblest, simplest gateway ever devised, the great wooden *torii*, standing, as it were, knee-deep in the sea. The giant leaning pines shade the never-ending line of

THE PINE-TREE

lanterns along the shore, their gnarled roots and trunks almost lapped by the waves; and here and there a twisted tree will seem to be hanging in mid-air, so slender does its root-hold look upon the cliff. The same eternal pines guard the little shrines all up the hill, and gather round the temple at the summit, from whence the prospect is the fairest man can see. Across the sea, as calm as a lagoon, so calm that it is hard to realise its surface is ever ruffled by winter storms, will rise other pine-clad islands, but surely none so fair as this.

The beauties of Lake Biwa, "a shell of mist and light," are sung universally. Constant reference is made in Japanese poetry to the eight views, known as the celebrated "Eight Beauties of Omi": the autumn moon seen from Ishiyama; the waning moon on Hiragama; the sunset at Seta; the evening bell of Miidera; the boats sailing back from Gabase; the bright sky with a breeze at Awazu; rain by night at Karasaki; and the wild geese alighted at Katata. If you examine these places, you will find that the pine-tree makes a background for most of them; and the rain by night would have no meaning if the pine-tree of Karasaki were not there. Probably this is the largest and most curious pine in the world; its great branches sweep outwards and downwards till they almost touch the ground, and, owing to the tree's great age, have to be supported by wooden props and stone cushions. A poet writes of the old Karasaki tree—

> There is a pine, a fount of age,
> Root cramped the land and sea between;
> Of mighty limbs, that curve and rage
> In eddying knots, and gusts of green.
>
> Its ancient trunk is lichen writ
> With autographs of centuries;
> The years, like sparrows, perch on it,
> And twitter plaintive memories.

As usual convention enters largely into this Japanese choice of especially lovely scenes, and probably were a foreigner asked to choose "Eight Beauties of Omi" he would name eight entirely different scenes. Certainly for one, I should choose the view from the top of the Castle of Hikone when the rice is still young and green, and the bloom of the honey-scented rape plant spreads broad stretches of yellow on the plains, forming a brilliant foreground to the lake beyond.

Next to Lake Biwa, although more properly speaking it is a lagoon, Lake Hamana is their largest lake, and here again the pine does so much in beautifying the whole scenery. Hamamatsu,

THE PINE-TREE

meaning the Pines of the Beach, is an historical place for pine-trees, and just beyond it lies the entrance to the lagoon; from the bridge can be seen on one side the breakers of the Pacific, and on the other the deeply indented shore line, clad with pine-trees, stretches away as far as the eye can see, while the mountains rise range upon range above the clear still water and form a picture dear to the heart of the poet.

If I were to tell you of all the places in Japan famous for their pine-trees, it would be one never-ending list, the pine is everywhere. If you travel along the sandy shore at Maiko or at Suma, across to the northern coast at Tsuruga, or at Maizuru, where the wonderful trees are of great antiquity, or back again to the coast near Kamakura, with the pine-clad island of Enoshima rising from the sea like a high green mass, through all the district of Hakone, or up north at Nikko, you will find the pine-trees,—no scenery can be parted from them; and if you are the happy possessor of a Japanese garden, the pine-tree will greet you at the gate.

Not only have the beauties of the pine been sung by poets for a thousand years, but they are also considered emblems of constancy, endurance, health, and longevity. The famous pines of

Takasago are well known as the theme of the *No* play in which the spirits of the pine-trees will appear as human shapes to celebrate the age of gold and happy life. The trees, with the colour of eternity and with their unexhausted life, are regarded as emblems of joy. It is the custom to sing a passage from this Takasago play at wedding ceremonies. The spirits of the two ancient pine-trees, personified as an old man and an old woman engaged in a never-ending task of raking up pine needles, are the subject, typifying longevity. The following is a passage from the play :—

The dawn is near, and the hoar frost falls on the pine-tree twigs; but its dark green leaves suffer no change. Morning and evening beneath its shade the leaves are swept away, yet they never fail. True it is that these pine-trees shed not all their leaves, their verdure remains fresh for ages long; even among evergreen trees—the emblem of unchangeableness—exalted is their fame to the end of time—the fame of the two pine-trees that have grown old together.

Their true poets seem never to tire of the pine, and it seems especially to appeal to the essentially poetical mind of the whole nation. In order to show me how it can be made the theme of poems and songs in conjunction with so many different subjects, a poet said to me, "It is simply wonderful to know what a good harmony the pine-tree

AZALEA AND PINE-TREE

keeps with other natural subjects; it harmonises with the misty spring moon, as well as with the summer moon. A well-known poem has been written on the pine-tree of the rainy season; and many poets sing of it together with the autumnal moon, and also it harmonises perfectly with the winter moon. You will find hundreds of poems written on the pines under snow; and the rain makes a beautiful combination with it also. It harmonises with mists, winds, and thunder lights; and you will see many pictures of the pine-tree and the rising sun. There is no better sight than to see it with the waves of the sea; and it goes well together with birds, with storks, pigeons, and with turtles or monkeys. The cuckoo will remind you of the pine-tree, and it makes a good subject with fire-flies and cicadæ." It is said that the pine is a brother of the plum and bamboo, and they make their appearance together in various forms on occasions of congratulation; and in conjunction with the crane and tortoise it is used in decoration to express the sentiment of happy old age.

The pine plays so large a part in the art of flower arrangement, so admirably described by Mr. Conder, that I cannot do better than quote some passages from the *Floral Art of Japan* in reference to the pine.

Flowers used at Moon-viewing

Moon-viewing is at all times a favourite pastime of the Japanese, but the great moon festival of the year is on the fifteenth day of the eighth month. The more important dwellings have a special chamber from which the sight of the moonlit landscape can be enjoyed. The floral arrangement occupies the recess of the chamber, and has of course no real connection with the outside prospect; but in the flower composition itself the moonlit landscape is expressed. A branch of a pine-tree is used, and between the *principal* and *secondary* lines of the composition a special branch is introduced, fancifully called the *moon-shadow-branch*; a hollow gap is also formed between the foliage, bounded by a special branch called the *dividing-branch*. In the composition the idea is to suggest both the opening through which the moon can be partially observed and the dark branch which appears to cross its surface. To fully appreciate the analogy one must be familiar with the scenery of Japan, and have seen, on a clear night, the irregular pine-trees standing out against the moonlit heavens.

We are told that the principal kinds of pine are the *Pinus Thunbergia*, known by the Japanese as the black or male pine; *Pinus densiflora*, called the red or female pine; and *Pinus parviflora*. There appear to be many different ways of arranging the pine branches, but in all cases they are left as much as possible in their natural state; a favourite treatment is that of a broad stump cut off horizontally, with a thick twisted branch springing from its base. *Pinus parviflora*, on account of the straightness and delicacy of its leaves, is often arranged in a simple vertical style, using the sprays; but for compositions with other species of the tree, thick gnarled branches are preferred. Mr. Conder also tells us of a pretty and poetical arrangement in connection with wedding ceremonies—

At wedding feasts a double arrangement in a pair of similar standing vases is employed. For this purpose a branch of the *male* pine is placed in one vessel, and a branch of the *female* pine in the other. The general form of each design would be similar, but the branch of the *female* pine facing the opposite vase should stretch a little beneath the corresponding branch of the *male* pine. These together are called the "Destiny-uniting" branches, and the complete design is said to typify eternal union.

In another passage he tells us how faithfully they reproduce the effect of the forest as—

Occasionally in suspended arrangements of pine, long stiff threads are hung from the branches, in conventional imitation of the parasitic grasses which attach themselves to this tree; and in disposing such threads, their balance into groups of three, five, or seven irregular lengths is carefully attended to.

Another very favourite form of fancy arrangement is called the "Fuji pine," as in such a composition a branch is bent to resemble the outline of Mount Fuji, and is combined with other branches and foliage in such a manner as to give the profile of the bare conical peak, and suggest at the same time the wooded country at its base.

Yet another form of pine decoration is the *Kadomatsu* or pair of gate pines, which are the most important decorations in front of every house at the New Year; the first seven days of the year are called *Matsu no uchi* or " Within the Pines." The origin of these *Kadomatsu* dates as far back as eight hundred and fifty years. One of the old *Kadomatsu* poets says—

> Kadomatsu no, itonami tatsuru sono hodoni
> Haru akegatatano yoya narinuran.
>
> (While busy decorating the pines at the gate,
> The dawn of the New Year speedily comes.)

The pines in front of the gates are placed in pairs—the rougher and more prickly one, called *Thunbergi* or male pine, on the left, which is the side of honour in Japan; the softer and more graceful one, *P. densiflora* or the female pine, on the right. The custom of adding bamboo is of more recent origin; and the other decorations include a rope, especially named *shimenawa*, with strips of

THE PINE-TREE

white paper, a cray fish, ferns, a large orange called dai dai, a leaf or two of an evergreen tree, dried persimmons, dried chestnuts, etc. Each one of these articles has its own peculiar origin, and is a symbol of good luck for the year and for life. The poet Ikku Zenzi writes—

> At every door the pine-trees stand,
> One mile-post more to the spirit land;
> And as there's gladness, so there's sadness.

And indeed, whatever the pine-trees at the gate may mean, it is for ourselves to choose whether we be happy or sad.

THE END

For Product Safety Concerns and Information please contact our EU representative GPSR@taylorandfrancis.com
Taylor & Francis Verlag GmbH, Kaufingerstraße 24, 80331 München, Germany